One Chapter at a Time

Reflections on Growth, Clarity, and Becoming

MANISH MANOHAR

One Chapter at a Time
Reflections on Growth, Clarity, and Becoming

First Edition: January, 2026

ISBN: 978-93-5635-879-9

Cover Design: Rehan Manohar

Interior Design & Layout: Abul Hussain Choudhury

Printed in India.

CONTENTS

PART II - GROWTH & ACTION

Introduction

One Chapter at a Time

This book was not planned; it unfolded — one chapter at a time.

What you are holding began as a simple daily practice. While preparing short videos for a private Facebook public-speaking group, I committed to reflecting on one idea each day. Every day brought a new topic, a new thought, and a new opportunity to pause and observe life as it was unfolding. I began jotting down these reflections simply to stay consistent with that commitment, never imagining they would one day take the form of a book.

Every chapter here is not only written by me — but lived by me. Over time, these reflections became a quiet compass, guiding my thoughts, decisions, and actions. Gradually, I noticed a shift — clarity replacing confusion, intention replacing hesitation, and growth emerging not from intensity, but from consistency.

The process was not easy in the beginning. Searching for ideas, filtering information, and shaping scattered thoughts into meaningful reflections was often challenging. But repetition changed everything. Reflection became a habit, and habit slowly turned into enjoyment. Writing one chapter at a time began to shape not just my content, but my character.

By showing up consistently—recording videos, reflecting daily, and continuing even on difficult days—I experienced a visible transformation. My speaking skills improved, my resilience strengthened, and my mindset evolved. Quiet discipline led me to take on greater responsibility, eventually becoming the President of a Toastmasters Club. Around the same period, after facing repeated setbacks, I qualified as a Cost and Management Accountant—reinforcing a lesson that appears often in these pages: progress comes from persistence, not perfection. Some of these reflections were also shared on my YouTube channel under my own name.

This book is not merely a collection of thoughts. It is a **101-day journey**, drawn from lived experience and shaped by repetition.

These 101 reflections have been carefully selected from **over 400 daily topics** on which I consistently shared my thoughts through short videos within that private group. Over time, certain ideas proved more enduring—returning again and again with relevance, depth, and quiet resonance across changing contexts. What remains in this book is not volume, but value: reflections chosen for their ability to slow the mind, clarify thinking, and gently support long-term growth.

To guide this journey meaningfully, the book has been structured into three parts, reflecting how growth naturally unfolds in life.

Part I — Self & Awareness focuses on understanding identity, choices, time, failure, and the beliefs that quietly shape our inner world. Before change becomes possible, awareness is essential.

Part II — Growth & Action moves from understanding to momentum. These reflections explore mindset, discipline, effort, relationships, and the courage required to keep moving forward consistently.

Part III — Wisdom & Life Design brings perspective. These chapters focus on balance, emotional strength, priorities, and living consciously with long-term clarity rather than short-term urgency.

You do not need to read this book in sequence. Each chapter stands on its own. Read one when life feels rushed, uncertain, or reflective. Let it sit with you. Return when you are ready for the next.

Many of the ideas in this book may feel familiar—we have heard them before. What changes everything is consistency. When reflection becomes a regular practice, small insights begin to compound. Thinking sharpens. Reactions soften. Decisions become more deliberate. These chapters may also serve as tools for conversation, public speaking, professional settings, classrooms, or any space where clarity of thought and expression matters.

This is my first book—unplanned, yet grounded in lived experience. It does not promise instant transformation. It promises something more reliable: steady growth and deeper clarity, built quietly over time.

If you are holding this book, it means the desire to grow already exists within you. All that remains is to pause, reflect, and move forward—**one chapter at a time**.

How to Read This Book

This book is not meant to be rushed.

One Chapter at a Time is a collection of short reflections, each designed to stand on its own. You do not need to read it from beginning to end, nor do you need to follow a fixed order. Read one chapter when you feel the need to pause, reflect, or regain clarity.

You may choose to read one chapter a day, letting the idea stay with you as you go about your life. Or you may open the book at any chapter that resonates with your current state of mind. There is no right way to read this book—only a conscious one.

The book is divided into **three parts** to gently guide you:

- **Self & Awareness** focuses on understanding your thoughts and choices.
- **Growth & Action** encourages consistency and forward movement.
- **Wisdom & Life Design** invites perspective, balance, and long-term clarity.

You are not expected to agree with every idea. Reflection is not about agreement—it is about awareness. If a chapter makes you pause or think differently, it has served its purpose.

Read slowly. Return when you are ready.

Let progress unfold—one chapter at a time.

— *Manish Manohar*

Day 1— You Are Your Own Limit

You are not limited by circumstances, people, or resources. You are limited only by your own mind. Every restriction you experience is first created in your thoughts. Fear of failure, fear of judgment, and fear of "what others will say" do not exist outside you—they live quietly within you. Most limitations are not real; they are imagined.

Many people live under the invisible weight of others' opinions. Society, criticism, and judgment appear powerful, but they have no physical existence. They gain influence only when you choose to give it to them. The moment you stop seeking approval, that power begins to fade.

Observe a two-year-old child. The child plays freely, falls repeatedly, gets up again, and keeps trying. There is no fear of failure, no concern about opinions, no hesitation. There are no limiting beliefs—only curiosity, courage, and joy. We are not born limited; we are trained to be limited.

Over time, our minds are conditioned by parents, teachers, society, and daily experiences. Gradually, beliefs are formed about what we can or cannot do. Many opinions offered by others are nothing more than borrowed self-limiting beliefs. When you accept them, they restrict your growth. When you question them, they lose their grip.

There is a story of an elephant tied with a small rope. When the elephant was young, the rope was strong enough to hold it. As the elephant grew, it became powerful enough to break free—but it never tried. It had learned to believe the rope still controlled it. Like the elephant, we are often not held back by real restraints, but by beliefs formed long ago.

The truth is simple and powerful: if you think you can, you can. If you think you can't, you can't. Your reality follows your belief.

Recognize a limiting belief, and you weaken it. Challenge it, and you expand your potential. You are your own limit—but once you realize this, you become limitless.

Break the rope. The strength was always within you.

Day 2 — Life Is Not About Finding Yourself, It's About Creating Yourself

Life is not something waiting to be discovered; it is something that must be created. You do not stumble upon a meaningful life by chance; you build it through consistent effort. What you become is not revealed to you—it is shaped by you.

When we are children, we are almost empty inside. We observe others, reflect, imagine possibilities, and slowly form ideas about who we want to be. Over time, through learning and effort, we shape ourselves into that vision. Life does not reveal who you are. Your actions do.

Creating yourself is not a one-time event; it is a continuous process. It requires daily hard work, continuous learning, the right attitude, guidance from the right mentors, and consistent practice. Each goal you achieve becomes a stepping stone toward the next, and with every step, you create a stronger, clearer version of yourself.

A sculptor does not find a statue hidden inside a stone. The statue is created through repeated effort—cut by cut, strike by strike. Every blow shapes the stone. Every mistake teaches the sculptor. Slowly and patiently, form emerges. In life, you are both the sculptor and the stone.

Life is the sum of the choices you make every moment, whether consciously or unconsciously. It cannot be "found"; it is shaped. There is no one else to blame. If life gives you lemons, you may complain—or you may choose to make lemonade. Ordinary effort leads to ordinary results. Creation demands intention.

Discipline builds destiny. Clear goals, consistent effort, mistakes, learning, and repetition—this cycle is what life truly is. As your knowledge grows, your horizon expands. When self-discipline joins hands with hard work, progress becomes inevitable.

If you want a better life, choose better in every moment—better habits, better thoughts, better actions. We are not victims of life. We are its creators.

Life is not about finding yourself—it's about creating yourself. And every choice you make is a brushstroke on the canvas of your life.

Day 3 — You Are the Product of Your Decisions

Every moment of life presents us with choices. What we choose in that moment becomes a decision, and those decisions—small and large—collectively shape the life we live. In each moment, we also have control over our thoughts. And since thoughts drive decisions, the quality of our life ultimately begins in the mind.

Thoughts are not random; they are choices. The way we think is influenced by our knowledge, values, beliefs, wisdom, and past experiences. Yet even these influences are outcomes of earlier decisions—how we spent our time, what we learned, whom we listened to, and how disciplined we were. In this sense, no one else is responsible for our thoughts. We are.

Life is not created by one big decision. It is built moment by moment—through daily actions, repeated choices, and consistent decisions. Even the way we think today is a mental habit formed by choices we made in the past.

Life often feels like standing at a Crossroads. There may be several paths leading to the same destination. You choose one, only to find yourself stuck in traffic, delayed and frustrated. Eventually, you may still reach where you wanted to go—but later than expected. Life works the same way. The path you choose determines how smoothly you progress, how many obstacles you face, and how much time and energy you lose along the way.

On the road, we rely on GPS, maps, or advice from someone who knows the route. In life, mentors act like a GPS, experience becomes the map, and learning from others helps us avoid unnecessary delays. Asking someone who has already walked the path can save years of effort and frustration.

Sometimes, while driving, we simply follow the car in front of us—only to end up stuck in the same traffic. We assume the driver ahead knows the best route, so we stop thinking for ourselves. Life works the same way. When we blindly follow others—their choices, timelines, or definitions of success—we often inherit their pressures and disappointments. What looks like progress may only be shared congestion.

Wisdom lies in pausing, observing, and choosing consciously. Not every road suits every traveler. Sometimes a different turn, though uncertain at first, leads to clarity and movement. Following the crowd may feel safe, but conscious direction is what truly moves you forward.

If careful thought is needed for a small driving decision, how can life's decisions be left to chance? Life is not meant to be lived on autopilot. Every moment is an opportunity to choose wisely.

You are the product of your decisions. Choose consciously—because every choice you make is shaping the life you will live.

Day 4 — Knowing Is Not Enough, We Must Apply

In today's digital world, knowledge is everywhere. We can search anything, watch countless videos, read articles, and learn theories within minutes. Most of us already know how to become successful, healthy, wealthy, and happy. Yet only a few actually achieve it. The reason is simple—knowing is not enough. We must apply.

Knowledge without action has no power. Knowing where water is stored will not quench your thirst. You must take a glass, pour the water, and drink it. In the same way, knowledge creates value only when it is applied consistently. We often read motivational quotes, watch inspiring videos, and admire successful people, but when it is time to act, we complain, blame circumstances, or focus on our weaknesses.

The knowledge we already possess is more than enough to move forward—if we use it. Life is not complicated; we make it complicated by ignoring application. As someone rightly said, *it doesn't matter how many resources you have if you don't know how to use them.*

This is why resolutions fail. We attend seminars, read books, and listen to podcasts, but if we do not decide what action to take within a few days, the motivation fades. Information remains information, and nothing changes. Without application, learning stays incomplete.

True learning happens only through action. We all went to schools and colleges, yet results vary widely. Those who move ahead are not always the ones with the highest marks, but the ones who apply what they learn. Many highly successful people were not academic toppers or even graduates. What separated them was not knowledge alone, but action.

Children do not learn to walk by reading rules. They learn by falling again and again. Retention increases only when knowledge is used. Knowledge without action is like bullets without a gun—powerful in theory, useless in reality. Action, even without perfect knowledge, is far better than perfect knowledge without action.

Use what you already know. Start where you are. Do what you can. Consistent action creates mastery, and failure teaches faster than theory ever can.

Knowing is not enough—we must apply. Because action is what turns information into transformation.

Day 5 — If You Respect Time, Time Will Respect You

Imagine a bank crediting ₹86,400 into your account every single day, with one condition—whatever you don't use is lost forever. You cannot save it, carry it forward, or recover it later. Would you waste even a single rupee? Of course not.

Your day works exactly the same way. Every day, life credits you with 86,400 seconds. Once they pass, they are gone forever. Time never refunds what you fail to use.

The value of time becomes clear only when it is lost. Ask a student who failed an exam what one year means. Ask a parent of a premature baby what one month means. Ask a daily wage earner the value of one day. Ask someone who missed a train what one minute means. Ask someone who escaped an accident what one second means. Ask an Olympic silver medalist what one millisecond means. Time waits for no one.

Life itself is made of moments, and moments are made of time. Time is the most limited resource we have, yet it is distributed equally to everyone. How far you go in life depends not on how much time you have, but on how well you respect it.

Respecting time is respecting your life. When you do not value your time, others will not value it either. If you do not learn to say no, others will fill your day with their priorities. Discipline begins the moment you protect your time.

Time quietly rewards responsibility and punishes carelessness. Those who respect time build focus, consistency, and self-respect—while those who waste it slowly give away their life, one moment at a time.

Time is non-renewable. Every second is an opportunity. Respect your time—and time will respect you.

Day 6 — Define Life Yourself

You are responsible for your own life. No one else defines it for you.

When we are born, we are completely raw. Over time, language, culture, upbringing, education, beliefs, and work begin to shape us. Yet everything we experience passes through one place—the mind. Our mind receives, processes, and interprets life based on our beliefs, attitudes, and understanding. Gradually, these perceptions become our personality. If we are the perceiver of everything that enters our life, how can anyone else define who we are?

Every moment, we are shaping ourselves. The words we speak, the thoughts we think, the food we eat, and the actions we take quietly influence who we become. Life is nothing but a series of choices. We choose whether to be polite or indifferent, whether to study or play, whether to work hard or just get by, whether to respond consciously or react impulsively. These small, daily choices define our character and determine the quality of life we experience.

Life does not simply happen to us—we attract what we allow and nurture. Circumstances may not always be in our control, but what we do next always is. To define something is to give it meaning and direction. We should never define ourselves by the chances given to us, but by the choices we consciously make.

Life is mysterious. Everything we experience—joy or misery, fear or peace—happens within us, not outside us. External situations are only triggers; the real experience is internal. That is why life feels light when we are happy and heavy when we are low. Its unpredictability is what gives it depth and power.

There is no fixed definition of life. We laugh freely like children, dream boldly in youth, think deeply with age, and care more gently as we grow. For a singer, life may be music. For an actor, expression. For someone else, service. Life is not about discovering a hidden definition—it is about creating one.

Life is a blank canvas, and you are the artist. You choose the colors. When you are clear about what matters, life gains direction. Without that clarity, it feels scattered and restless. The meaning of life also changes with time, and that is natural.

Life is not about avoiding failure; it is about how gracefully you treat it. Failure refines life—it does not ruin it. When you treat failure with dignity, success eventually honors you.

Life is a challenge—meet it. Life is a gift—accept it. Life is an adventure—dare it. Life is love—enjoy it. Life is an opportunity—take it.

Life doesn't come with a definition. You write it—every single day.

Day 7 — Accept the Failure, but Don't Accept Not Trying

Failure is often called the key to success, and rightly so. If you have never failed, it simply means you have never truly tried. Failure is not an interruption in life—it is part of the journey. Out of fear of failure, many people stop trying altogether. And when life stops moving, growth stops with it.

Success in the game of life is impossible without action, and every action carries the risk of failure. Failure does not mean you are incapable; it means you dared to act on an opportunity instead of standing still.

Every failure is a teacher. When we learn from failure, we grow stronger, wiser, and more resilient. As long as we are true to our purpose, success and failure should be treated the same way—as feedback. Losing is not the opposite of winning; it is part of winning. When you fall, the only task is to get up and keep moving forward. Only by trying do you discover how far you can go. As Albert Einstein said, *"Failure is success in progress."*

Mastery in anything demands repetition, and repetition always includes failure. A great swimmer improves by swimming again and again. A great pianist masters music by practicing the same scales repeatedly. There is no escape from repetition. The more you repeat an action, the better you become at it. Failure is not a dead end—it is a redirection. It shows you where not to go and nudges you toward a better path.

Failure also builds maturity. It gives us the chance to pause, reflect, and return with better judgment. Never trying is far worse than failing, because it denies you the full experience of life. Everyone fails at some point; it is not something to fear—it is a natural process of growth. Thomas Watson Sr. once said, *"The fastest way to succeed is to double your failure rate."* Confucius reminded us, *"Our greatest glory is not in never failing, but in rising every time we fail."* Failing to fail is what truly keeps a person stuck.

Failure hurts—and that is okay. Pain should be felt, not suppressed. When emotions are accepted, they pass faster and leave less damage behind. When ignored, they return later as anger, sadness, or frustration. Failure should be reflected upon honestly: what went well, what didn't, and what can be improved next time. Reflection turns pain into progress.

History offers countless reminders that failure is not the end. Many people who later changed the world were rejected, ignored, or dismissed repeatedly before succeeding. Failure did not stop them—quitting would have.

Failure is proof that you tried. Not trying is the only real failure.

Accept failure with courage— but never accept a life where you didn't try.

Day 8 — When You Become 80 Years Old, What Will Matter to You

When I turn eighty, what I want most is peace—peace with the life I lived and the person looking back at me in the mirror. I do not want to carry regret for a life half-lived, for courage withheld, or for choices postponed. I want to know that I lived honestly, fully, and bravely.

At that stage of life, what will truly matter will not be money or status, but family—the people who stood by me through every season. What will matter is whether I lived my life to the fullest, whether I pursued the dreams that once kept me awake with excitement, and whether I contributed something meaningful to the world around me. It will matter that I lived with dignity, independence, and self-reliance—free in body, mind, and spirit.

Turning eighty will mark the beginning of life's final chapter. In that moment, I would want to look back without "if only" and "what if." I would want to feel that my life was worth living—not perfect, but purposeful.

By then, certain truths will stand clear. What will matter is not what I bought, but what I built. Not what I got, but what I gave. Not success, but significance. Not how much I learned, but how much I shared. What will matter most are the quiet acts of integrity, compassion, courage, and sacrifice—the moments when I lifted someone else, encouraged them, or made their journey a little lighter.

Character will matter more than credentials. It will not matter how many people I knew, but how many feel my absence. It will not matter what memories I carry, but what memories others carry of me. How I am remembered—and why—will define my legacy.

A life that truly matters does not happen by accident. It is not shaped by circumstances, but by daily choices. Every day, we choose whether to live consciously or carelessly, courageously or comfortably. These small choices, repeated over time, quietly decide whether life feels fulfilled or wasted.

Choose today to live a life that will still matter to you when you are eighty.

Day 9 — Use It or Lose It

The mind decides what is important based on use. When we learn something new but fail to apply it, the brain quietly begins to discard it. Information that is not used is treated as unnecessary. That is why practice, repetition, and application are not optional; they are essential.

Research shows that we forget a large portion of what we learn within hours, and even more within a day, if it is not applied. This forgetting has nothing to do with intelligence, age, or motivation. Knowledge or skill that is not used simply fades away. What we use stays. What we ignore disappears.

This is the law of use. Anything that is not used over time loses its strength or effectiveness.

Nature reflects this truth clearly. Ostriches were once birds that could fly. Over time, because they stopped using their wings for flight, they lost that ability. The same law applies to human beings. Whatever we do not use—our skills, health, time, knowledge, ideas, courage, or opportunities—slowly weakens.

Every person is born with unique abilities, just like a fingerprint. Many may have similar talents, but how you use yours makes it distinct. These talents are like diamonds buried within us. No one else can dig them out for us. Once discovered, they must be polished through effort, practice, and care. The more we invest in nurturing our abilities, the more value they bring—to us and to others.

Life is not a race to win or a competition to survive. It is a privilege and a responsibility. We are entrusted with abilities and resources not to store them safely, but to use them meaningfully. What we use grows. What we neglect fades.

You can discover your natural strengths by asking simple questions: What excited you as a child? When do you lose track of time? What do you deeply yearn to become? These answers often point toward what is meant to be used.

This law applies not only to skills, but to courage, ambition, hope, dreams, and vitality. Whatever we do not use does not remain neutral—it weakens. Whatever we continue to use and nurture multiplies.

Use your gifts boldly— because whatever you don't use, you eventually lose.

Day 10 — Organize Your Mind

To organize your life, you must first organize your mind. Everything you experience, clarity or confusion, peace or chaos—begins with your thoughts. When the mind is scattered, life feels scattered. When the mind is organized, life begins to fall into place.

Thoughts arise largely through language. While the mind thinks in images, language gives those images meaning, direction, and emotion. Language was created to communicate with others, but over time it also became the way we speak to ourselves. If this inner dialogue is left unmanaged, it can create confusion, anxiety, and unnecessary suffering.

An unorganized mind reacts automatically. It overthinks, jumps to conclusions, and magnifies problems. An organized mind responds consciously. It pauses, chooses wisely, and acts with clarity. Organizing the mind does not mean suppressing thoughts—it means learning to manage them.

Emotions are a powerful part of the mind. Sadness, anger, fear, and anxiety are natural, but when they remain unchecked, they begin to control our actions. Emotional balance returns when we move the body, take a walk, exercise, breathe deeply, or simply pause before reacting. Emotion is energy, and movement helps regulate it.

Attention is the foundation of mental organization. A distracted mind feels noisy and restless. A focused mind feels calm and strong. When you stay present, listen fully, and keep your attention on what matters, mental clutter reduces naturally. Where attention goes, energy flows.

When thoughts are organized, decisions become easier. When emotions are regulated, clarity emerges. When focus improves, productivity and peace follow without force. An organized mind is not loud, it is clear, calm, and deliberate.

Organize your mind first; everything else will align naturally.

Day 11 — Challenges Are Essential for Success

Challenges are what make life interesting, and overcoming them is what gives life meaning. Problems are not interruptions in life—they are an essential part of it. Every challenge carries an experience, a lesson, and an opportunity to grow. Each one quietly shapes us into who we are becoming.

Everyone faces difficulties. No one is exempt. What separates people is not the absence of challenges, but the way they respond to them. The way you face problems defines your character, resilience, and ultimately, your success.

Real growth rarely happens in comfort. Comfort teaches very little. Struggle, on the other hand, teaches deeply. Challenges force us to learn new skills, rethink old patterns, and discover inner strength we didn't know existed. Just as a diamond is formed under immense pressure, human beings grow stronger, wiser, and more conscious through difficulty.

Many of life's storms feel unfair when we are in them. But when we look back, those very moments often stand out as turning points. Challenges are placed in our path not to break us, but to build us.

We all face common struggles—fear, self-doubt, the opinions of others, lack of motivation, setbacks, rejection, and moments of lost control. How we handle these moments determines how far we go.

There is a story of a butterfly struggling to emerge from its cocoon. When someone tried to help by cutting it open, the butterfly survived—but it never learned to fly. The struggle was necessary. The resistance strengthened its wings. Without it, the butterfly was weakened. In the same way, removing struggle from life would rob us of strength.

If life removed all challenges, we would never develop

resilience, courage, or depth. Adversity is not only inevitable—it is necessary. Often, challenges arrive disguised as rejection, failure, or hardship, but hidden within them are lessons that prepare us for greater heights.

Challenges teach us that we are stronger than we think. They cultivate gratitude and compassion. They clarify what truly matters. They sharpen grit and persistence. And when success finally arrives, it feels meaningful only because struggle came first.

Don't wish for an easy life. Wish for the strength to rise through challenges and fly.

Day 12 — Logic Will Take You from A to B, Imagination Will Take You Everywhere

Logic helps us move from one known point to another. It works within facts, figures, and evidence. Logic connects dots that already exist, but it rarely creates new ones. It stays within what is proven, measurable, and familiar, keeping us safely inside established boundaries.

Imagination has no such limits.

Every breakthrough in human history began not with logic, but with imagination. First, someone imagined what did not yet exist. Only later did logic step in to organize, test, and execute the idea. Logic arranges ideas; imagination creates them.

The human mind works through two complementary forces. One side seeks structure, analysis, and reason. The other dreams, visualizes, and explores possibility. Logic is restricted to what is already known. Imagination ventures into the unknown. Without imagination, knowledge would never expand.

Imagination is powerful because it gives birth to knowledge itself. It makes life interesting and colorful—through music, stories, art, and invention. A world without imagination would be efficient, but empty. Every innovation we admire today was once nothing more than a thought in someone's mind, dismissed by many as unrealistic or impossible.

Imagination also has the unique ability to travel instantly. In a single moment, it can take us across time, space, and future possibilities. When life brings failure, rejection, or uncertainty, imagination allows us to picture a better tomorrow—and gives us the strength to keep going.

Yet imagination alone is not enough. Balance is essential. Logic keeps us grounded and realistic. Imagination keeps us creative and bold. Logic is the brake; imagination is the accelerator. Progress requires both. Without imagination, we never move forward. Without logic, we lose control.

Living purely by logic is like being a tourist in life—following fixed routes, visiting popular destinations, ticking boxes, and observing from the outside. Living with imagination is like being a traveler—open to detours, exploring the road less taken, and experiencing life from the inside out. Tourists follow the path. Travelers create their own journey.

Use logic to move forward— but use imagination to discover where to go.

Day 13 — Sometimes Not Getting What You Want Is a Wonderful Stroke of Luck

Sometimes in life, no matter how deeply we want something or how hard we work for it, life seems determined to deny us. It feels unfair, as if luck has turned against us. In those moments, disappointment feels personal—and painful.

But what appears as bad luck is often an opportunity in disguise. It is life's way of nudging us toward a different road—often a better one. We may never know what worse fate our apparent bad luck saved us from. What feels like loss today may be quiet protection.

When life takes something away, the pain can feel unbearable. Explanations sound hollow. We tell ourselves that everything happens for a reason, yet that reason feels invisible in the moment. Days pass, sorrow deepens, and clarity feels far away. But time has a way of revealing what emotions cannot see. What once felt like rejection slowly reveals itself as redirection.

Life does not deny us things to punish us. It does so to expand us, reshape us, and push us toward growth we did not yet imagine. Often, it is through disappointment that we become stronger, wiser, and more self-reliant. We begin to create our own luck.

When we look back honestly, many moments we once labeled as "bad luck" turn out to be blessings. Paths that closed forced us to explore new ones. Comfort zones broke, new skills emerged, and new versions of ourselves were discovered. As someone once said, many rejections are simply redirections to something better.

Some doors close because they are not meant for us. Some close because we are meant to open them later. And some close so that we can find doors leading to something far more meaningful. Life often sees further than we can.

Disappointment carries hidden gifts. It removes fear when there is nothing left to lose. It realigns focus when plans fail. Small progress after failure builds confidence. Lessons learned prevent future mistakes. Discipline grows even without applause. Effort continues without recognition. Inner strength expands—and once you rise from hardship, very little feels impossible.

Sometimes life saying no is the luckiest thing that can happen—because it is guiding you toward something better than you imagined.

Day 14 — Your Team Is Your Reflection

Your team is not shaped primarily by instructions—it is shaped by observation. People learn most powerfully not from what leaders say, but from what leaders do. This learning happens quietly, subconsciously, and continuously.

If a leader understands their role deeply and performs with discipline, commitment, and integrity, the team beneath them often reflects the same qualities. Leaders are the custodians of culture. What they tolerate, practice, and repeat becomes the norm.

If you want punctuality, respect for time, and accountability in your team, you must demonstrate these qualities first. When your team sees that you honor your own commitments, they naturally become more careful with theirs. Values are not enforced—they are absorbed.

The quality of a team is a direct reflection of its leader. When a team is underperforming, the most uncomfortable but honest place to look is the mirror. Great leaders understand this truth and take responsibility for it. Leadership gaps show up as team gaps.

If there is behavior in your team that troubles you, ask yourself first whether you are modeling the same behavior. Leaders are role models by default. If you want accountability, you must show accountability. If you want openness and trust, you must practice openness and trust. You cannot steer your team's ship if you cannot first steer your own.

Emotions flow downward. Optimism and pessimism spread fastest from the top. If a leader is stressed, angry, or reactive, the team absorbs tension and uncertainty. If a leader is calm, patient, and encouraging, the team gains confidence and stability. Every organization eventually reflects the emotional tone of its leadership.

This truth applies beyond offices—to parents, coaches, mentors, and guides of every kind. Example is always louder than instruction. Actions speak when words fall silent.

Your team will reflect what you consistently show them. Make sure the image looking back at you—from the mirror of your organization—is the one you truly want to see.

The strongest leadership message is not spoken—it is lived.

Day 15 — Don't Cry Over Spilt Milk

We don't need to stress over the small mistakes of the past. Life moves forward, not backward, and each new day offers a fresh opportunity to begin again. Letting bygones be bygones does not mean forgetting what happened—it means refusing to let past errors control our present emotions.

Most mistakes, when viewed from a distance, are far smaller than they feel in the moment. Worrying about them does not change anything. When milk has been spilled, it cannot be poured back into the cup. Crying over it only wastes time and energy. The wiser choice is to clean up, learn the lesson, and move on.

Holding on to the past drains emotional strength that could be used far more constructively. Acceptance brings peace. Once we accept that something cannot be undone, our mind becomes free to focus on what lies ahead rather than what lies behind.

I experienced this lesson personally when my young son unknowingly downloaded a paid app, resulting in an unexpected deduction from my bank account. My first reaction was irritation. But anger would not reverse the transaction. Instead, I chose to treat it as a learning moment—for him and for myself. We spoke about responsibility, made changes to prevent a repeat, and moved on. Peace returned the moment acceptance replaced frustration.

This is the essence of the saying "Don't cry over spilt milk." It reminds us that worrying about what cannot be changed only adds to our suffering. When something goes wrong and no repair is possible, the best response is acceptance, learning, and forward movement.

Every setback carries a lesson. Those lessons, when embraced, help us avoid repeating the same mistakes. What matters is not what happened, but how we respond to it.

Learn from the past. Let go of regret. Focus on what you can control—your response, not what's already gone.

Day 16 — To Just Win, Go Solo; To Dominate, Go With a Team

Winning alone is possible—but domination is rarely a solo act. True greatness is built through collective effort.

When the Avengers defend the Earth, no single superhero saves the day alone. Each brings a unique strength, and together they become unstoppable. That is the essence of teamwork. Success is not just about individual brilliance—it is about how well strengths are combined toward a shared goal.

There is a reason the saying exists: it's not the team with the best players that wins, but the players with the best team. Great achievements in business and life are almost never created in isolation. They are built by people who learn to work together.

Consider The Beatles. Four individuals with different personalities and talents came together, balanced one another, kept egos in check, and created music that changed the world. Together, they became far greater than the sum of their individual abilities. That is what effective teams do—they multiply impact.

Talent may win games, but teamwork and intelligence win championships. Individual effort can take you far, but a strong team takes you further than you ever imagined. When people collaborate, respect differences, and share responsibility, the possibility of long-term success increases dramatically.

Nature quietly teaches the same lesson. Migrating geese fly in a V-formation to reduce resistance and conserve energy. They rotate leadership when one gets tired. They encourage one another from behind. And when one is injured, others stay back to support it. The group moves forward because no one is left behind. Ants, too, carry loads far heavier than themselves—together.

From sports teams and orchestras to workplaces and families, the principle remains unchanged. A single person can achieve only so much. But when people unite around a shared purpose, support one another, and move forward together, they reach heights that would be impossible alone.

Go solo if you want a quick win. Go with a team if you want lasting dominance.

Day 17 — Knowledge vs Experience

Knowledge and experience are closely related, yet they are not the same. Knowledge can be taught, explained, and transferred. Experience cannot. It must be lived, felt, and realized personally.

Knowledge lives in the mind. Experience lives through the senses. Knowledge helps us understand something intellectually, but experience allows us to truly know it. You can read about something, talk about it, and even explain it—but until you experience it, your understanding remains incomplete.

A child may have many experiences but little knowledge. Parents provide knowledge so the child can make sense of those experiences. As we grow, this relationship continues. Knowledge gives structure, but experience gives depth. Knowledge without experience often leads to ego, assumptions, and shallow understanding. Experience, on the other hand, grounds us in reality.

If you see a fruit and name it, that is knowledge. But when you taste it, only then do you truly know it. Knowledge gives labels; experience gives meaning. Knowledge exists in memory, while experience becomes part of who you are.

You may read about Paris and know everything about it, but visiting Paris is a completely different understanding. Reading ten books on meditation may make you knowledgeable, but practicing meditation over time makes you wise. Knowledge may tell you how to fly a plane, but only sitting in the cockpit reveals whether you truly can.

Knowledge is like a map. Experience is the journey. The map is useful—it shows direction—but it cannot replace walking the path. Growth happens when knowledge is put into action. Wisdom is born not from knowing, but from doing.

There was an experiment where one group studied pottery

for months before making a pot, while another group started making pots from the very first day—failing repeatedly and learning through practice. In the end, the best work came from those who learned through experience. Failure refined their skill; action shaped mastery.

Knowledge is important—but experience completes it. Knowledge is theory. Experience is reality.

Learn what you can—but don't stop there. True understanding begins when knowledge turns into experience.

Day 18 — Adversities Bring Opportunities

A certain amount of adversity in life is not just inevitable—it is necessary. Kites rise against the wind, not with it. In the same way, human beings rise not despite difficulties, but because of them. Those who accept adversity as a challenge do more than survive—they grow stronger, wiser, and reach heights they could not have imagined before.

Adversity reveals opportunity to those willing to look for it. As the saying goes, a pessimist sees difficulty in every opportunity, while an optimist sees opportunity in every difficulty. What feels like resistance is often the very force that lifts us upward.

History quietly confirms this truth again and again. Periods of scarcity, crisis, and hardship have often triggered the greatest transformations. When resources ran low, innovation emerged. When systems failed, stronger ones were built. What once looked like collapse later revealed itself as reinvention.

There is a proverb that says, when it is darkest, we may see the stars. Problems and challenges are not dead ends; they are platforms for expansion. Struggle sharpens courage. Setbacks build character. Many of the strongest leaders and most meaningful breakthroughs were forged in difficult times.

Adversity introduces us to ourselves. In moments of comfort, we rarely question who we are or what we are capable of. In moments of difficulty, those questions become unavoidable. That is when true strength, resilience, and values reveal themselves.

Recent global challenges reminded us of what truly matters. They forced us to slow down, spend time with ourselves, learn new skills, rethink careers, value family, respect everyday work, and embrace technology. What began as disruption quietly created new ways of thinking, working, and living.

Adversity, beneath its harsh exterior, is an invitation—to adapt, to grow, and to evolve. When met with courage and optimism, every difficulty carries within it the seed of opportunity.

Adversity is not a roadblock— it is a stepping stone. Rise against the wind, and you will rise higher than before.

Day 19 — Life Is Not What You Get, It Is What You Make It

Life is not something handed to us—it is something we create. Circumstances may shape the setting, but they do not write the story. We are not defined by what happens to us; we are defined by how we respond. What we can always control are our actions, thoughts, attitude, determination, learning, the company we keep, and the habits we build.

Life is like a deck of cards. You don't choose the cards you're dealt, but you always choose how you play them.

If we observe people who have achieved lasting success, we notice a common pattern. Their lives were not easy, but they were intentional. Faced with hardship, they chose effort over excuses and belief over bitterness. Two people may face the same difficulty—one gives up, the other rises. The difference is not the situation; it is mindset and choice.

Consider Amitabh Bachchan, who rebuilt his career after financial crisis and rejection through discipline and resilience. A. P. J. Abdul Kalam rose from a humble childhood to lead a nation through education and perseverance. Nawazuddin Siddiqui worked as a watchman while chasing his craft before recognition arrived. Vijay Shekhar Sharma faced rejection and financial instability before building a fintech giant. Milkha Singh transformed poverty and personal loss into legendary achievement.

Others echo the same truth. Smriti Irani began working young amid financial strain and rose through persistence. B. R. Ambedkar confronted untouchability and reshaped society through courage and education. Across the world, figures like Dwayne Johnson and Sachin Tendulkar faced early setbacks yet chose consistency and belief.

Coal under pressure becomes a diamond. Pressure does not destroy—it reveals strength.

Life rewards responsibility. When you stop blaming circumstances and start owning your choices, momentum shifts. Difficult beginnings often lead to powerful endings—not by chance, but by commitment.

Life is not what you get— it is what you make it. When you take responsibility for your actions, life begins to change in your favor.

Day 20 — Old Ways Won't Open New Doors

Everything in life is a result of the choices we have made so far. If we want a different outcome, we must make a different choice. If we want something new, we must be willing to do something new. Nothing improves until we improve.

As Albert Einstein famously observed, doing the same thing over and over again and expecting different results is insanity. The habits, beliefs, and actions of yesterday have created the life we live today. If we want a better tomorrow, today must look different.

There are new places life can take us and new experiences waiting to be lived. But we cannot step into new doors carrying old beliefs. Often, we assume our beliefs are true simply because they are familiar. We use them to interpret the world—without questioning whether they still serve us.

Unlearning is just as important as learning. Some beliefs that once helped us may now be holding us back. Just because something worked in the past does not mean it is the best way today. Growth often begins the moment we are willing to challenge what we think we already know.

Trying to open a new door with an old key will never work. In the same way, new opportunities demand new thinking and new action. The world does not change first—our perception of it does.

Life is filled with possibilities waiting to be discovered, but discovery requires courage. If we keep doing the same things, we keep getting the same results. If we want something we have never had, we must be willing to do something we have never done.

Old ways won't open new doors. Change your thinking. Change your actions. And watch new paths appear.

Day 21 — Fortune Favours the Brave

One who never plays cannot win the game. Courage is not about taking reckless risks or chasing fortune blindly—it is about showing up despite fear. Fortune does not reward foolishness; it rewards bravery in action.

Fear itself is not the enemy. It is one of our most basic human instincts, designed to protect us from danger and alert us to risk. Fear helps us pause, assess, and stay alive. In fact, the absence of fear in genuinely dangerous situations is not strength—it is dysfunction. Fear, in its true form, exists to protect us.

But fear has a shadow side. When misunderstood, it becomes an invisible chain. Instead of guarding us, it traps us. It stops us from trying, from risking failure, from putting ourselves out there, and from pursuing the life we truly want. The same instinct meant to save us can end up shrinking us.

Courage does not mean the absence of fear. Courage means the willingness to move forward while fear is present. It means facing the fear of mistakes, failure, judgment, rejection, embarrassment, and responsibility—and acting anyway.

Fear is like a warning sign on the road. It is meant to slow us down and make us alert, not force us to stop completely. When we acknowledge fear instead of running from it, growth begins. Each time we act despite fear, its grip weakens. With repetition, what once terrified us becomes manageable—and eventually familiar.

This is where courage is rewarded. Fortune, in this sense, means success. Success comes to those who step into uncertainty, accept change, and persist beyond fear. It does not come to those who wait safely on the sidelines. Life does not reward stillness—it rewards movement.

Some of the greatest milestones in history were achieved by people who felt fear deeply, yet refused to let it decide their future. They faced setbacks, failures, and criticism—but they kept moving forward.

Fear will always whisper reasons to stop. Courage listens—and moves anyway.

Fortune does not favour the fearless. It favours those who act despite fear.

Day 22 — Things Cartoon Characters Taught Us

Cartoon characters may look simple, but behind the humor and innocence lie powerful life lessons. If we observe closely, they quietly teach us how to live better, happier, and more meaningful lives.

Spider-Man teaches us responsibility. Power—whether talent, money, or knowledge—brings lasting happiness only when it is used for others.. Helping people multiplies growth, just as protecting the city gave meaning to his strength.

Mickey Mouse reminds us that attitude is everything. Life is like music—if you focus only on mistakes, you miss the rhythm. Smiling through difficulty doesn't remove problems, but it makes them easier to face.

Mr. Bean shows that happiness is a choice. He finds joy in the smallest moments, proving that happiness does not depend on perfection or possessions, but on mindset.

Tom and Jerry teach us about relationships. Despite constant conflict, they cannot live without each other. True bonds may clash, but they survive disagreements and stand the test of time.

Doraemon teaches the value of friendship. Good friends don't abandon you when you fail—they guide you, support you, and help you grow into who you are meant to be.

Cartoons entertain us as children, but their lessons guide us for life—if we choose to notice them.

Power gains meaning when shared. Attitude lightens life. Happiness is a choice. Relationships outlast conflict. And good friends shape destiny.

Day 23 — When You Come Out of the Storm, You Won't Be the Same Person

Every life passes through storms. Some are visible—failures, losses, sudden changes. Others are silent—fear, confusion, emotional pain, inner conflict. These storms may not always be physical, but they are real, and they are unavoidable.

The storm is not meant to destroy you. It is meant to transform you.

Growth rarely comes from comfort. It is born when life pushes us to our limits—when certainty disappears and we are forced to confront ourselves honestly. Pain becomes the teacher. Struggle becomes the classroom.

Life's storms are like fire to metal. Fire burns and reshapes, but when the metal emerges, it is stronger and more resilient than before. In the same way, adversity refines us. It removes what is unnecessary and strengthens what truly matters.

Failure teaches humility and resilience. Heartbreak brings emotional depth and clarity. Difficult phases often become turning points—moments where maturity is born and perspective changes.

When you walk out of a storm, you may not recognize yourself. That is not loss—it is growth. The person you were could not have survived what the person you are now has endured. The storm leaves marks, but those marks are not signs of weakness; they are proof of survival.

You don't come out untouched. You come out wiser.

The storm does not ask for permission, but it leaves behind wisdom. When you walk out of it, you don't return as who you were— you arrive as who you were meant to become.

Day 24 — You Don't Solve a Problem by Worrying

Worry doesn't solve problems. It only creates noise.

At its core, worry is an attempt to control what we cannot control. We worry about the economy because we can't control it. We worry about our children because we can't fully protect them. We worry about the future because it is unknown. Worry is the mind's way of trying to manage uncertainty—but it never succeeds.

Worry begins when the mind jumps into the future and imagines negative outcomes. These imagined scenarios are rarely facts; they are stories created by fear. Worry is not reality—it is a state of mind.

Worrying is like sitting in a rocking chair. It gives you something to do, but it doesn't take you anywhere.

Worry does not stop bad things from happening. It only stops you from enjoying the good that is already present. Some level of worry is natural—we all worry about exams, interviews, finances, or important conversations. But when worry becomes constant and uncontrollable, it starts draining energy, clarity, and peace.

Chronic worry creates the illusion of control. We tell ourselves that by thinking through every worst-case scenario, we are preparing. In reality, we are exhausting ourselves. Worry replaces action with anxiety and solutions with speculation.

The real shift happens when we move from worrying to problem-solving. Most worries feel external, but they are internally fueled by our self-talk. When we worry, we repeatedly rehearse feared outcomes instead of addressing what we can actually do.

Action breaks worry. Movement interrupts anxious loops.

Sharing concerns lightens the mental load. Calm breathing settles the nervous system. Problem-solving begins when the mind is quiet enough to think clearly.

Worry feels productive—but it produces nothing.

You don't solve a problem by worrying about it. You solve it with clarity, calm thinking, and action.

Day 25 — If It's Not Okay, It's Not the End

Everything will be okay in the end. And if it's not okay, it's not the end.

No matter who you are or what you are going through right now—financial stress, broken relationships, confusion, or a sense of being stuck—remember this phase will pass. What feels heavy today is not permanent. It is a moment in your journey, not your destination.

Struggles are not punishments. They are signposts. They point us toward growth, maturity, and deeper understanding. Even when life feels unfair or unclear, it is quietly shaping you into someone stronger and wiser.

Every heartbreak, disappointment, and setback carries a lesson. You may not see it while you are in the middle of the pain, but time reveals what emotion hides. What feels unbearable now often becomes the very reason you grow later.

Life is like an obstacle race. There are sharp turns, moments of exhaustion, and times when quitting feels tempting. But the finish line exists. The journey is not meant to be smooth—it is meant to be meaningful.

Patience is essential. Everything has an end, even the hardest seasons. When the end arrives, things often begin to make sense. Pieces fall into place in ways we could not imagine earlier.

Life moves in cycles—ups and downs. Growth is rarely straight or predictable, but it is always forward. If nothing feels okay right now, remind yourself of this truth: the story is still being written.

Not okay is not the end. It is just the middle of the journey.

Day 26 — Converting Weaknesses into Strengths Is Success

No one is good at everything. Every individual carries weaknesses—but the people who succeed are not those without flaws; they are those who learn how to deal with them wisely. Success is not about pretending weaknesses don't exist. It is about converting them into strengths—or at least ensuring they don't hold us back.

We cannot change the cards we are dealt in life, but we can always choose how we play the hand.

Having weaknesses is not the problem. Everyone has them. What truly matters is how we respond. When life hands us limitations, excuses keep us stuck, but effort turns obstacles into opportunities.

There is often confusion about whether we should focus on strengths or weaknesses. The truth is both matter. We should play to our strengths—but we must also work on our weaknesses enough so they don't slow us down. A weakness ignored can quietly become a brake on progress.

Think of it like driving a car with the handbrake slightly pulled. No matter how hard you press the accelerator, the car won't move smoothly. Improving weaknesses is like releasing that handbrake—it allows your strengths to work freely.

The first step is honesty. You cannot fix what you refuse to acknowledge. Once you accept a weakness, preparation becomes your strongest tool. Preparation builds confidence and reduces fear. The more prepared you are, the less power your weakness has over you.

You also don't have to do everything alone. Leveraging other people's strengths is not a flaw—it is intelligence. Delegation and teamwork allow you to move faster and further.

Many weaknesses persist only because we avoid them. When faced regularly, fear fades and competence grows. Every expert was once a beginner who chose to practice instead of hide.

You don't need to be great at everything. You only need to be good enough to move forward. **Jack Ma** did not know programming or how to build a website, yet he understood technology well enough to build a team and create something extraordinary.

Sometimes improving weaknesses brings greater results than endlessly polishing strengths. Progress beats perfection.

Converting weaknesses into strengths is true success. Never let self-doubt or limitations stop you from becoming who you can be.

Day 27 — Even a Correct Decision Is Wrong If It Is Taken Too Late

It is often better to make a wrong decision quickly than to make a right decision too slowly. No amount of overthinking can guarantee the perfect choice. Time waits for no one—and in many situations, delay itself becomes the biggest mistake.

A fire extinguisher used five minutes late is useless, even if it is the right tool.

Opportunities are time-bound. In a fast-moving world, speed matters. Many ideas fail not because they are bad, but because they arrive too late. Someone else acts first. Someone else captures the moment. Waiting quietly turns possibility into regret.

Successful people decide quickly and adjust along the way. Unsuccessful people delay, avoid, or wait for certainty that never comes. Procrastination is often fear wearing the mask of caution.

There is no perfect time. There is no perfect decision. Only hindsight tells us whether a choice was right. Waiting for all the traffic lights to turn green before driving will keep you parked forever.

Progress favors action. Consider how **Virgin Atlantic** entered the airline industry—decisively, without knowing everything. They moved first, learned fast, and adapted. Had they waited for complete certainty, they would never have taken off.

Most decisions are reversible. If a choice can be corrected at low cost, make it and refine later. Act quickly when risks are small. Movement creates clarity—standing still creates none.

Perfectionism is the enemy of progress. Endless analysis drains energy that could be used to move forward. You don't learn to swim by standing at the pool's edge—you learn by getting in.

A delayed right decision can be worse than a quick wrong one. Because movement—right or wrong— always moves you forward.

Day 28 — You Have Done It Before, and You Can Do It Now

There are moments when nothing feels positive—when self-doubt grows loud and confidence feels distant. In those moments, pause and look back. Remember the times you faced difficulty and still moved forward. Those moments are proof that you are capable, even when you temporarily forget it.

Confidence is like a battery. When it runs low, it doesn't mean it's broken—it only needs recharging. And the best way to recharge it is by remembering the times it already powered you through challenges.

Sometimes, the reassurance we seek from the world must come from within. Learn to speak kindly to yourself during low moments. The way you talk to yourself matters. Gentle, encouraging self-talk restores focus and helps you find direction again.

Never allow circumstances or people to define your worth. You are unique, and comparison only weakens confidence. A diamond does not lose its value just because it lies among stones.

Instead of replaying failures, revisit your achievements. What you have done well in the past is evidence of what you can do again. A student who remembers earlier success finds the courage to try once more instead of giving up.

Life is not a race against others. It is a journey with yourself. Compete only with your past self. Growth happens when you honour your own path and progress at your own pace.

You were born unique. Just as no two fingerprints are the same, no two life journeys are identical. Treat yourself with patience and kindness. When confidence feels low, do something small that reconnects you with who you are.

Strength returns when self-belief returns.

You have done it before, and you can do it now. Trust yourself—your past is living proof of your strength.

Day 29 — Take Care of the Minutes, and the Hours Will Take Care of Themselves

The people who use time most effectively are not those who chase big hours—they are those who respect small minutes. A productive life is not built in grand gestures, but in how carefully we handle the ordinary moments of each day.

We often complain that we don't have enough time, yet we overlook the value of the minutes quietly passing by. Every day offers the same number of minutes to everyone. The difference lies in how we use them.

A building is not constructed in a day—it is built brick by brick. In the same way, a meaningful and productive life is built minute by minute.

The way we engage with small moments slowly shapes how we engage with life itself. Small improvements, repeated consistently, lead to powerful transformations. In elite sports, the difference between winning and losing often comes down to a tiny margin—just 1% or 2% extra focus, effort, or discipline. That edge is created by paying attention to small details every day.

The same applies to life. A student who studies with focus for 30–40 minutes daily often outperforms someone who studies for long hours irregularly. Consistency beats intensity.

How we spend our days determines how we spend our lives. And how we spend our minutes determines how our day unfolds. Yesterday, last week, and last year all passed one moment at a time.

Time never waits. It cannot be stored, saved, or recovered. Like flowing water, it can only be used while it moves.

You don't find time—you make time. Great outcomes are built

from small units: One word builds a book. One grain builds a meal. One drop builds an ocean. One second builds a day.

Excellence is nothing more than careful attention to small moments, practiced daily.

Take care of the minutes, and the hours will take care of themselves. Greatness is built in many well-used moments.

Day 30 — The Best Things in Life Are Free

Money can buy many things—but they remain just that: things. Material possessions may offer comfort and convenience, but they cannot guarantee happiness. The most meaningful aspects of life do not come with a price tag.

You can fill a house with expensive furniture, but warmth comes only from the people inside it.

The moments that truly nourish us are free. A warm hug. A shared smile. Laughter that lightens the heart. Time spent with friends and family. Feeling loved, accepted, and understood. These are the experiences that sustain emotional well-being and bring lasting joy.

The trap of materialism is subtle. New clothes, gadgets, or possessions may create a brief sense of excitement, but that feeling fades quickly. What endures are relationships, memories, and moments of connection. Life is not about collecting things—it is about collecting experiences.

Memories are photographs of the heart. You don't buy them; you live them.

Nature reminds us daily that the best gifts cost nothing. Sunrises and sunsets. A cool breeze on a warm day. The fragrance of flowers. The sound of birds or waves. These simple experiences are priceless, yet freely available to all.

Kindness, too, costs nothing. A smile, a gentle word, or a helping hand can change someone's day—and often our own. Positivity multiplies when shared.

Happiness is not hidden in what we own, but in what we notice and appreciate.

The best things in life are free. Slow down, notice them, and let gratitude do the rest.

Day 31 — The Most Important Thing You Wear Is Your Personality

People form impressions faster than we realize—often within just a few seconds. While clothes may draw attention, it is personality that creates connection. You may change outfits every day, but the way you make people feel stays with them long after the moment has passed.

Personality is the invisible outfit you wear at all times. It shows in how you walk into a room, how you listen, how you respond under pressure, and how you treat those who can do nothing for you. Your tone of voice, eye contact, posture, facial expressions, and choice of words quietly communicate who you are—even when you are silent.

True personality is not about being flashy, loud, or dominant. It is about presence. Confidence without arrogance. Warmth without pretence. Strength without aggression. A calm and respectful demeanour often speaks louder than expensive clothing or polished appearances.

People rarely remember exact details of what you wore, but they remember how comfortable they felt around you. They remember whether you were kind, attentive, confident, and genuine. That emotional imprint is what builds trust, influence, and long-term relationships.

A strong personality is built from within. It grows through self-awareness, emotional intelligence, integrity, and consistent behaviour. When your inner values align with your outward actions, authenticity becomes effortless—and authenticity is always attractive.

Think of personality like a fragrance. You cannot see it, but everyone notices it. And just like fragrance, it lingers even after you leave.

The most important thing you wear is your personality. Dress it every day with confidence, kindness, and authenticity—because that is what truly defines you.

Day 32 — A Problem Is a Chance for You to Do Your Best

If we observe successful people closely, one common trait stands out among all of them. It is not luck, talent, or resources—it is mindset. They look at problems differently. Where most people see obstacles, they see opportunities to learn, adjust, improve, and rise stronger than before.

A problem, in truth, is not an interruption in life. It is an invitation. Like a rough stone that appears ordinary at first, a problem reveals its value only when it is polished through effort, thinking, and persistence. What looks like trouble today often becomes wisdom tomorrow.

When we develop this mindset, our mental energy automatically shifts. Instead of worrying about how bad the situation is, the mind begins searching for solutions. Such people do not waste time complaining, blaming, or panicking. They ask better questions. *What can be done? What can be learned? How can this be turned around?* That shift alone changes everything.

Viewing problems positively reduces stress. Panic fades because the mind moves from fear to planning. Clarity begins to emerge as the problem is broken into smaller, manageable parts. Each solved problem strengthens confidence and prepares us for bigger challenges ahead. Even failure feels lighter, because it is no longer defeat—it becomes feedback.

Very often, the real problem is not the situation itself, but our attitude toward it. When we focus only on problems, they multiply in our mind. When we focus on possibilities, opportunities begin to appear. Successful people understand this deeply. They know that creativity is born under pressure, and innovation often comes from difficulty.

There are people who complain when it rains—and there

are those who learn how to collect water. When a flight gets cancelled, most people get angry. A few look around, observe the situation, and ask how the same problem affecting everyone can become an opportunity. That difference in thinking is what separates average outcomes from extraordinary ones.

Every challenge demands a new way of thinking. As Albert Einstein wisely said, *"We cannot solve our problems with the same thinking we used when we created them."* Problems push us to expand our perspective, sharpen our intelligence, and discover strengths we did not know we had.

Each problem you face is training you. It is shaping your patience, resilience, creativity, and confidence. It is preparing you for a higher version of yourself.

A problem is a chance for you to do your best. Because every challenge you face is shaping who you are becoming.

Day 33 — Victory Is Sweetest When You Have Known Defeat

Only those who have tasted defeat can truly understand the real value of victory. When we study the lives of great and successful people, one truth becomes clear—they were not born winners. They stumbled, failed, and were defeated many times along the way. What separated them from the rest was not an absence of failure, but the refusal to surrender to it.

Victory feels sweetest when it comes after the hardest battles. The struggle sharpens patience, strengthens perseverance, and builds inner resilience. Without the journey through loss, success feels shallow. With it, success feels earned.

Think of water after a long period of thirst. Its taste is incomparable. In the same way, victory after defeat carries a depth of satisfaction that effortless success never can.

It is often said that if you want to understand victory, ask the one who has lost—not the one who has always won. Defeat teaches lessons that success alone never can. It humbles us, grounds us, and forces us to grow. Success achieved without failure may bring comfort, but it rarely brings wisdom.

Life itself exists in contrasts. Light has meaning because of darkness. Joy is understood because sorrow exists. Heat is appreciated because of cold. In the same way, success derives its meaning from failure. One cannot be fully understood without the other.

A person who has never struggled often takes success for granted. But someone who has fallen, failed, and risen again carries gratitude, humility, and strength within them. They value every win because they remember the pain of loss.

Failure does not weaken us—it prepares us. Every setback trains the mind, tempers the spirit, and builds the character required to handle success responsibly. Rising after defeat is where true growth occurs.

Victory is sweetest when you have known defeat. Because only those who have fallen truly understand the joy, strength, and meaning of rising again.

Day 34 — Let Success Become Your Addiction

Success has a quiet power—it creates more success. Every achievement, no matter how small, builds confidence and fuels the desire to move forward. When we experience progress, even in small doses, something shifts inside us. We begin to believe more. We begin to expect more. Momentum is born.

Success is like climbing a staircase. Once you reach one step, the next no longer feels impossible—it feels closer.

Many people admire "overnight success," forgetting that it usually takes years of effort hidden behind the scenes. Success rarely arrives suddenly. It is built slowly, through discipline, repetition, patience, and countless invisible hours of work. What truly matters is not speed, but direction—and the courage to keep moving.

Success becomes addictive because it rewards effort. Like a video game, you clear one level, feel the satisfaction, and immediately want to try the next. Each win—however small—releases motivation. You become more focused, more energetic, and less distracted. This is a healthy addiction, one rooted in growth rather than escape.

Small wins deserve celebration. When you acknowledge progress, you reinforce the habit that created it. Discipline followed by appreciation teaches the mind that effort is worthwhile.

Fuel a fire regularly, and it keeps burning. Ignore it, and it fades.

Success does not come from dramatic actions taken once—it comes from simple actions repeated daily. Discipline turns effort into habit, and habit turns success into a way of life. Over time, consistency compounds. Tiny improvements multiply into extraordinary results, just as small investments grow through compound interest.

To become addicted to success, begin with action. Movement creates clarity. Choose your environment wisely, because ambition grows faster when surrounded by people who value progress. Start small, but stay consistent—momentum will do the rest.

Take time to acknowledge your wins. Speak about them. Own them. What we think about, talk about, and celebrate, we naturally repeat.

Let success become your addiction. Because once you fall in love with progress, growth becomes unstoppable.

Day 35 — Don't Try to Change Others

In every human life, real change happens organically. It does not arrive because someone demanded it, advised it, or forced it. Change happens only when a person feels ready from within. No one truly transforms because they are told to—people change because they *want* to.

You can change yourself, but you cannot change others. And interestingly, when you change yourself—your attitude, your behaviour, your responses—your world begins to change. Often, people around you seem different, not because they changed, but because *you did.*

You cannot force a flower to bloom by pulling its petals. It blooms only when the season is right.

Trying to change others almost always fails because it ignores a basic truth: external pressure creates resistance, not transformation. Telling someone to quit a habit they do not want to quit rarely works. Advice given without readiness falls on closed ears.

Change imposed from the outside rarely lasts.

If someone's behaviour troubles you, you really have only two healthy choices. You can accept them as they are, or you can create distance. Trying to reshape someone into a version you prefer is unfair—to them and to you. Acceptance brings peace. Distance brings clarity. Control brings frustration.

More often than not, what we dislike in others reflects something unresolved within us. Instead of fixing people, it is far more effective to work on our own mindset and behaviour. When we change internally, our interactions soften naturally.

When you clean the mirror, the reflection improves on its own.

As Mahatma Gandhi reminded us, *"Be the change you wish to see in the world."* Growth begins inward. Energy spent judging or correcting others is better invested in emotional maturity, self-awareness, and personal discipline.

Boundaries play a quiet but powerful role here. Knowing what you will tolerate—and what you will not—is not selfish. It is self-respect. Boundaries do not push people away; they simply define where you stand.

A fence does not block people—it defines space.

Don't try to change others. Change yourself—and watch how everything around you begins to shift naturally.

Day 36 — Happiness Is a Choice, Not a Result

Happiness is not something we arrive at after achieving enough, earning enough, or becoming enough. It is not a destination waiting at the end of effort and ambition. Happiness begins much earlier. It begins the moment we decide to be content with what we have, right where we are.

Happiness does not come from circumstances, possessions, or success. It comes from an inner decision. Nothing external has the power to make us happy unless we allow it. Searching for happiness outside ourselves is exhausting, because happiness was never missing—it was only postponed.

Happiness is like a switch within us. No matter how bright the world outside appears, the light turns on only when we choose to flip the switch. Our peace cannot be taken from us unless we hand it over. Thoughts, emotions, and responses belong to us, and how we experience life depends on what we choose to hold inside.

History offers powerful reminders of this truth. Even in extreme suffering, human beings retain one freedom—the freedom to choose their attitude. When this realization settles in, circumstances lose their control over us. Life may be unfair, painful, or disappointing at times, but our emotional response remains our responsibility.

Many people unknowingly give this power away. They blame the past, other people, or situations for their unhappiness. Yet while we cannot control everything that happens to us, we can always control how we respond to it.

Happiness does not arrive "one day." It exists now—in the way we think, speak, and interpret life. People are as happy as they decide to be. Those who choose joy do so not because life is perfect, but because they refuse to postpone peace.

Simple daily choices strengthen this habit—gratitude over complaint, acceptance over resistance, presence over regret. When we stop fighting life and start living it, happiness quietly finds its place.

Happiness is not a reward. It is a choice. Choose it daily—especially when life gives you reasons not to.

Day 37 — What You Get by Achieving Your Goals Is Not as Important as What You Become

Goals give direction to life, but they are not the final reward. The true value of a goal lies not in what it gives you at the end, but in who you become while pursuing it. Achievements may bring money, titles, or recognition—but character, discipline, and inner strength are the real prizes earned along the way.

The destination may offer a view, but the journey builds the strength to reach it.

While chasing a goal, something subtle yet powerful happens within you. You begin to wake up earlier. You learn to say no to distractions. You develop patience when results are slow and courage when fear shows up. These qualities do not disappear once the goal is achieved—they stay with you for life.

A student preparing for a competitive exam may or may not succeed on the first attempt. But the habits formed—focus, consistency, resilience—become lifelong assets. Even if the goal changes, the growth remains.

Results are temporary. Growth is permanent.

A trophy can be lost, replaced, or forgotten. But the discipline built through effort becomes part of your identity. Goals are not meant to define your worth; they exist to stretch you beyond comfort and shape a stronger version of yourself.

When you focus only on outcomes, disappointment is inevitable. When you focus on becoming better, every step has value—even setbacks. A goal that makes you more disciplined, humble, and resilient has already fulfilled its true purpose.

What you become while achieving your goals matters more than the goals themselves. Because results may fade—but growth stays forever.

Day 38 — Don't Let Yesterday Take Up Too Much of Today

Yesterday is already over. No matter how often we replay it in our minds, it cannot be changed. Yet many people allow yesterday's mistakes, regrets, and disappointments to occupy today's mental space—stealing energy from the only moment where change is possible.

Driving while constantly looking in the rear-view mirror will eventually cause an accident.

The past often carries weight—guilt over mistakes, pain from rejection, regret over missed chances. Reflection is healthy, but living there is harmful. The past is meant to teach, not to imprison.

A student who keeps reliving a poor exam performance loses focus for the next one. Another who learns from it and moves forward grows stronger. The difference is not intelligence—it is attention.

Today is where your power lives.

You cannot rewrite yesterday's page, but you can write today's chapter beautifully. Growth begins when you stop feeding yesterday with today's energy. Holding on to the past often feels safe because it is familiar—but familiarity should never be confused with progress.

Forgiving yourself is not weakness. It is wisdom. Letting go does not erase the lesson—it frees you to move forward.

When you choose action over regret, yesterday naturally loosens its grip. Progress begins the moment your focus returns to the present.

Don't let yesterday take up too much of today. Learn from the past—but live, act, and grow in the present.

Day 39 — Success Doesn't Come to You, You Go to It

Success is not something that arrives on its own. It does not knock on the door of those who wait, wish, or hope. Success belongs to those who take initiative—those who move toward it with intention and consistent action.

You don't catch a train by standing still on the platform. You have to move, step forward, and board it.

Many people dream of success while waiting for the perfect conditions—complete confidence, total clarity, or someone else's approval. But successful people understand a simple truth: confidence is built *after* action, not before it. Waiting feels safe, but it quietly delays growth. Movement, even when imperfect, attracts progress.

Action creates opportunity. Opportunities rarely appear first and then invite us in. More often, they reveal themselves only after we begin moving. A job seeker who learns new skills, applies consistently, and reaches out creates far more openings than someone who waits passively for the "right chance." Effort opens doors that waiting never will.

Excuses keep people stationary. Effort moves them forward.

Success belongs to those who show up daily, put in focused work, and refuse to quit when things become uncomfortable. A parked car, no matter how powerful, cannot reach any destination. Direction matters—but movement matters more.

To find success, you must go where it exists. You must build the right skills, place yourself in the right environments, and surround yourself with people who value growth. Success lives at the intersection of preparation and action.

You don't need giant leaps to get there. Small steps, taken consistently, still move you forward. Even the longest journey begins with a single step—and continues one step at a time.

Success doesn't come to you, you go to it. Move with purpose, and success will meet you on the way.

Day 40 — The Secret of Getting Ahead Is Getting Started

Most people do not stay behind because they lack talent, intelligence, ideas, or resources. They stay behind because they never truly begin. The greatest barrier to progress is not difficulty—it is hesitation. The hardest part of any journey is always the first step. Once that step is taken, momentum begins to form, and what once felt overwhelming slowly becomes manageable.

A car stuck in one place needs enormous energy to move. But once it starts rolling, even gentle pressure keeps it going. Life works the same way.

Fear thrives on delay. The longer we wait, the more intimidating a task becomes. Our mind exaggerates effort, risk, and consequences. But the moment we act—even in the smallest way—fear begins to shrink. Action has a calming effect. It replaces imagination with reality.

A student afraid of studying often feels paralysed by the size of the syllabus. Yet the moment the book is opened and ten minutes of reading begins, resistance reduces. The mind settles. Progress replaces panic. This is because action creates clarity, while inaction creates doubt.

Many people wait endlessly for the perfect plan, perfect mood, or perfect timing. But perfection is a trap. It looks intelligent, but it silently delays growth. You don't learn to swim by analysing water—you learn by stepping in. Progress has never required perfection; it has always required participation.

Big results rarely come from big beginnings. They come from small, repeated starts. One page read, one task completed, one call made—these simple actions may feel insignificant, but they create momentum. And momentum changes everything.

Once you start, effort feels lighter. Confidence grows naturally. What once looked impossible begins to look doable. Like a small snowball rolling downhill, tiny actions gather strength as they move forward.

You don't need more time, more resources, or more confidence to begin. You only need the willingness to start with what you already have, where you already are.

The secret of getting ahead is getting started. Begin now—and let momentum take care of the rest.

Day 41 — Insecurity Kills More Dreams Than Failure Ever Will

Everyone experiences insecurity at some point in life. It is not a personal flaw or a sign of weakness—it is a natural response to living in an uncertain world. Self-doubt, fear, frustration, anger, or a vague sense of groundlessness arise not because something is wrong with us, but because life itself offers no guarantees.

Feeling insecure is not the real problem. Insecurity is part of being human. The real damage begins with how we respond to it.

Insecurity rarely arrives loudly. It works quietly, almost invisibly. We begin to hesitate. We delay. We overthink. We withdraw. Sometimes we become defensive or rigid. Sometimes we distract ourselves with busyness, screens, or emotional numbness. At other times, we abandon possibilities before they even begin. These reactions may soothe discomfort for a moment, but over time they quietly erode confidence, courage, and momentum.

At its core, insecurity is rooted in uncertainty. Outcomes are never fully within our control—careers, relationships, finances, results, and even how others perceive us. The mind senses this uncertainty first in the body, then translates it into thoughts of inadequacy or fear. Waiting for an answer, feedback, or results can trigger insecurity even when we have done our best.

The instinct to escape insecurity only strengthens it. Avoidance, self-criticism, blame, or emotional withdrawal feel protective, but they reinforce fear. Trying to outrun insecurity is like trying to outrun your shadow—it follows wherever you go.

Insecurity cannot be eliminated. It must be faced.

When we learn to stay with insecurity instead of fighting it, its grip loosens. Like waves in the ocean, it overwhelms only when resisted. When allowed to rise and fall, it passes.

One rule matters most: never act from insecurity. Pause before responding. Let the emotion settle. Many regrets are born not from bad intentions, but from insecure reactions.

Failure teaches. It strengthens. Insecurity does not. Failure may knock you down—but insecurity keeps you from standing up.

Insecurity ends more dreams than failure ever will. Learn to stay present with discomfort, act with awareness, and your dreams will outlast what insecurity tries to destroy.

Day 42 — Believe It's Always Day One

Every journey in life begins with a goal. A goal gives direction—it tells us where we want to go. But direction alone is never enough. The distance between intention and achievement is crossed only through action, taken one step at a time.

Most people do not fail because they lack dreams. They fail because they hesitate at the starting line.

We plan. We visualise. We imagine outcomes. Yet when the moment to act arrives, we wait. We wait for confidence to appear, for clarity to settle, for conditions to feel perfect. We tell ourselves we will begin "soon." But unless we begin, nothing moves. And when nothing moves, even the most beautiful destination remains unreachable.

Success is rarely delayed by difficulty. It is delayed by waiting.

The longer we postpone the beginning, the farther our goals drift away. Day One does not arrive someday in the future. Day One arrives the moment we decide. In life, there are only two choices: *one day* or *day one*. And the distance between them is the distance between dreaming and doing.

Waiting for the perfect time is one of the most convincing traps of the mind. It feels sensible, even responsible—but often it is fear disguised as preparation. Waiting for everything to align is like sitting in a car and refusing to start because every traffic signal ahead is not green. You will remain parked forever.

Most dreams quietly fade in a place called *tomorrow*.

Planning has value. It gives direction and structure. But overplanning becomes a sophisticated form of procrastination. A map can guide the journey—but staring at the map forever will never move your feet. At some point, planning must turn into motion.

The first step is always the hardest. But it is also the most powerful. The moment you take it, fear loosens its grip, clarity improves, and momentum begins to build.

Jeff Bezos often describes Amazon as a "Day One company." His belief is simple: the moment an individual or organisation starts behaving as if it has arrived—comfortable, slow, risk-averse—it begins to decline. Day Two is stagnation, followed by irrelevance.

Day One thinking keeps you alert, hungry, and willing to learn. It carries the energy of beginnings—the first day of a new job, the first step into the unknown, the start of something meaningful. There is effort. There is focus. There is openness.

When you believe it is always Day One, you stop waiting for motivation and start creating momentum.

Believe it's always Day One. Because the journey does not begin when you feel ready—it begins the moment you decide to start.

Day 43 — Not Taking Help Can Hold You Back

Asking for help often feels uncomfortable. We fear it might make us appear weak, incapable, or dependent. Sometimes we worry about being judged. Other times, we are afraid of hearing a simple "no." Yet the truth is far gentler than our fears: most people genuinely like helping. It makes them feel useful, trusted, and connected.

Ironically, it is not asking for help that holds us back—it is refusing it.

No meaningful success is achieved alone. Behind every visible achievement stands invisible support. Athletes have coaches. Leaders have mentors. Creators have collaborators. Even the strongest individuals rely on others at critical moments. Trying to do everything alone is like rowing a boat with one oar—you move, but you circle endlessly instead of moving forward.

Courage, like strength, grows through use. The first time you ask for help, it may feel awkward. The second time, slightly easier. Over time, what once felt frightening becomes natural. Growth always lies on the other side of discomfort.

When you ask for help, you are not burdening someone—you are giving them an opportunity to contribute. Think of how it feels when someone trusts you enough to ask for guidance. It feels meaningful. It feels human. Asking for help is not selfish; it is relational.

It also reveals truth. Anyone can claim to care, but support is proven through presence. Asking for help clarifies relationships and shows you who genuinely stands with you.

Carrying everything alone creates unnecessary stress. Humans are wired for connection, not isolation. When responsibility is shared, emotional weight lightens. A burden carried together feels smaller—not because it disappears, but because you are no longer alone with it.

Many dreams are delayed simply because we don't know where to start. Asking for help turns confusion into clarity. Guidance breaks procrastination. Fear shrinks when someone walks beside you.

Avoiding help to protect pride is costly. Learning matters more than appearing capable. High performers understand this. They actively seek advice, feedback, and perspective—not because they are weak, but because they want to grow.

Vulnerability, though feared, is often perceived as strength. We judge our own vulnerability harshly, while admiring it in others. Asking for help signals honesty, courage, and self-awareness.

Growth does not happen in isolation. It happens in conversation, collaboration, and connection.

Not taking help doesn't make you strong—it keeps you stuck. Growth begins the moment you are brave enough to ask.

Day 44 — If You Chase Two Rabbits, You Will Not Catch Either One

This old proverb carries a simple truth that many people learn the hard way: divided attention leads to divided results. When your focus is scattered, your energy is diluted. And when energy is diluted, progress slows to a standstill.

Most of us don't fail because we lack ability or opportunity. We fail because we try to do too many things at once.

Focus is the quiet force behind every meaningful achievement. You can accomplish almost anything in life—if you give it your full attention. Excellence demands commitment, patience, and the courage to say no to distractions. When all your effort flows in one direction, momentum becomes inevitable.

Think of sunlight. Spread across a wide field, it only warms the ground. But when the same sunlight is focused through a lens, it can ignite fire. Nothing changes except concentration.

There is a beautiful lesson in the way a crane hunts. Standing still at the water's edge, it does not rush at every movement. Small fish pass by. The crane waits. If it grabs at everything, it gains nothing. If it wants the big fish, it must allow the small ones to go. Focus requires patience—and restraint.

Life constantly offers small temptations and side opportunities. Chasing all of them feels productive, but it often pulls us away from what truly matters. A student who tries to prepare seriously for an exam while juggling multiple unrelated pursuits usually ends up exhausted and average at all of them.

You cannot chase two big dreams running in opposite directions. Each demands a different mindset, skill set, and level of commitment. Catch one rabbit first. Then, if you choose, go after the next.

Many talented people fall short not because they lack skill, but because they keep switching paths. Meanwhile, those with ordinary talent but extraordinary focus often rise far higher. Digging ten shallow holes will never find water. Digging one deep well will.

Focus builds mastery. Skills sharpen. Confidence grows. Results compound. Focus is not about doing more—it is about doing less, better.

Chase one rabbit. Catch it. Then decide if you want another. Because focus is what turns potential into achievement.

Day 45 — Willpower Is a Muscle: Exercise It Often

Behind almost every meaningful achievement lies a quiet but decisive force—willpower. Talent may open doors and motivation may spark beginnings, but it is willpower that keeps a person moving forward when enthusiasm fades, when distractions multiply, and when comfort whispers excuses. Willpower is what allows us to stay disciplined, build habits, and act in alignment with our long-term goals rather than our short-term impulses.

At its core, willpower is the ability to choose what is right over what is easy. It is the strength to delay gratification—to endure a little discomfort today for a better life tomorrow. Every time you resist temptation, stay focused, or complete a task despite resistance, you are exercising this inner strength.

What makes willpower powerful—and manageable—is that it works just like a muscle. When you use it regularly, it grows stronger. When you avoid using it, it weakens. And when you push it without rest or support, it becomes fatigued. This is why self-control feels harder late in the day or during periods of stress. The brain consumes energy when exercising discipline, and when that energy runs low, temptations feel louder.

This understanding removes self-blame. Struggling with discipline does not mean you lack character—it often means your willpower muscle is tired or undertrained.

The way forward is not extreme discipline, but consistent training. Small, repeated acts of self-control are the most effective way to build lasting willpower. Waking up on time, finishing what you start, choosing focus over distraction, or sticking to a routine even when it feels boring—these are daily workouts for the mind.

Just as physical strength is not built by lifting the heaviest weight on day one, mental strength is not built by demanding perfection overnight. Start small. Be patient. Increase difficulty gradually. Over time, discipline becomes natural, and what once required effort begins to feel effortless.

Willpower also needs support. Adequate sleep, nourishing food, physical movement, and structured routines help conserve and restore mental energy. A disciplined life is not created through force alone, but through intelligent self-care.

Willpower is not something you either have or don't have—it is something you train. Use it daily, strengthen it gradually, and support it wisely. Because disciplined effort today creates freedom, confidence, and control tomorrow.

Day 46 — Never Compromise Your Happiness

The most important relationship you will ever have is the one you have with yourself. You may care deeply for others, support them, and wish them well—but none of that should come at the cost of your own happiness. You cannot truly offer love, patience, or strength to others if you are constantly empty inside.

Many people turn self-sacrifice into a way of life. They ignore their own needs, silence their emotions, and carry responsibilities that were never meant to be theirs. Over time, this leads to exhaustion, resentment, and a quiet loss of self. Helping others is meaningful, but setting yourself on fire to keep others warm is not kindness—it is self-neglect.

Your happiness is not optional. It is not selfish. It is essential.

When your inner state is healthy, life begins to move differently. A peaceful mind makes clearer decisions, handles pressure with balance, and recovers faster from setbacks. Productivity improves not because you force yourself harder, but because inner resistance fades. A happy mind works with life, not against it.

Happiness also has a quiet magnetism. When you are genuinely content, you naturally attract healthier relationships and better experiences. You can only give what you already possess. Just as you cannot pour water from an empty glass, you cannot share peace or joy if you deny them to yourself.

Happiness does not come from external circumstances. Life is imperfect by nature, and conditions are always changing. Waiting for everything to be right before allowing yourself to be happy is a promise that will never be fulfilled. This does not mean you will never feel sadness, fear, or disappointment. These emotions are part of being human. But they do not have to define your life. Happiness is not the absence of problems—it is the ability to remain grounded despite them.

Choosing yourself does not require apology. Saying no when needed, walking away from emotional harm, protecting your mental space, and choosing peace over constant conflict are acts of self-respect. This is your life. You are responsible for protecting its quality.

Think of happiness as the fuel for your journey. Without it, even the most impressive destination leads to burnout. Happiness is not found by accident—it is practised daily, through awareness, boundaries, and self-respect.

Never compromise your happiness. Because a life lived without inner joy is a life lived on someone else's terms—and you deserve better than that.

Day 47 — Perfection Doesn't Exist

Perfection assumes a world without error. Without cracks. Without mistakes.

In other words, a world without humans.

Perfection does not exist—and the sooner this truth is accepted, the lighter life becomes. What we often call perfection is not excellence; it is anxiety dressed up as discipline. It feeds the fear of not being enough, the fear of disappointing others, and the fear of being seen as flawed.

Perfection is fool's gold. From a distance, it shines. Up close, it dissolves.

People spend years chasing it—polishing, correcting, delaying—only to realise that the finish line keeps moving. There is always something more to fix, something more to refine, something more to fear.

Perfectionism does not improve performance. It quietly destroys it.

It delays action. It suffocates creativity. It keeps ideas locked away because they are "not ready yet."

Work remains unfinished not because of lack of ability—but because of fear disguised as standards.

Perfectionism is like waiting for perfect weather before starting a journey. You keep waiting, adjusting plans, checking forecasts—while life continues moving forward without you.

We are often taught that perfectionism means pride in work, attention to detail, and high standards. But there is a difference between caring deeply and demanding flawlessness. High standards encourage growth. Perfectionism demands impossibility.

As Maria Shriver observed, *"Perfectionism doesn't make you feel perfect; it makes you feel inadequate."*

At its core, perfectionism is fear wearing a respectable mask. Fear of failure. Fear of criticism. Fear of being exposed.

Research consistently shows that those trapped in perfectionism hesitate more, take fewer risks, and progress slower—not because they lack talent, but because they are afraid to begin imperfectly. Meanwhile, others move forward, learn from mistakes, and grow stronger through action.

Letting go of perfection is not lowering standards. It is reclaiming power.

Growth requires mistakes. Creativity requires imperfection. Progress requires movement.

You do not grow by being flawless. You grow by being honest enough to try.

Life is not asking you to be perfect. It is asking you to be real.

Let go of perfection. Choose truth over illusion, progress over paralysis, and courage over fear. Because evolution begins the moment you stop trying to be flawless—and start allowing yourself to grow.

Day 48 — Our Thoughts Create Our Experiences

Our thoughts create our experiences.

If you want to change what is happening outside you, you must first look at what is happening inside you. Life does not happen randomly. It unfolds in response to the patterns running silently through the mind.

What you think influences how you feel. How you feel influences how your body responds. And how your body responds influences how you act in the world.

Action, repeated over time, becomes experience.

This is why two people can live in the same circumstances and yet experience life completely differently. The difference is not the situation—it is the thought behind it.

Thoughts, by themselves, have no power. They are neutral events, like clouds passing through the sky. But the moment you give a thought your attention, it begins to feel real. That attention fuels emotion. Emotion drives behaviour. Behaviour shapes outcomes. And those outcomes then appear to "prove" the original thought.

A cycle quietly forms:

A thought appears. Attention locks onto it. Emotion arises. Action follows. Experience reinforces belief.

Over time, this loop hardens into a mindset. What began as a passing idea slowly becomes a way of seeing life.

This is why many of our problems are not problems of circumstance, but problems of perception. Failing in business is not the real problem. The real problem is the meaning you assign to that failure. Disliking your job is not the core issue.

The story you repeatedly tell yourself about what that job says about your worth is.

We do not suffer because of events. We suffer because of how we interpret events.

Most people try to change life from the outside in—new jobs, new cities, new relationships—without realising that experience is always projected from the inside out. As long as the inner narrative remains unchanged, the outer scenery may shift, but the feeling of life stays the same.

If you repeatedly think, *"I am not good enough,"* you will feel inadequate, you will behave defensively or cautiously, and your results will mirror that belief—confirming it once again.

This is how beliefs trap us.

Once a belief forms, the mind begins working selectively. It looks for evidence that supports the belief and quietly ignores evidence that contradicts it. Over time, repeated thoughts turn into beliefs. Beliefs solidify into identity. And identity shapes reality.

Yet here is the most liberating truth: You are not your thoughts. You are the one who notices them.

Thoughts are not facts. They are suggestions. They pass through the mind constantly. They only gain authority when you cling to them, argue with them, or identify with them.

Imagine your mind as a farm. Thoughts are seeds blown in by the wind. Some seeds grow flowers. Some grow weeds. You cannot stop seeds from arriving—but you absolutely decide which ones you water. Attention is the water. Whatever you nourish grows stronger.

Change does not begin with force or suppression. It begins with awareness.

When you start observing your emotions, your bodily reactions, and the thoughts you repeatedly feed, something shifts. This awareness—thinking about your thinking—breaks the automatic loop. You begin to notice patterns instead of being ruled by them.

And in that noticing, choice returns.

You don't change your life by fighting your thoughts. You change your life by no longer believing every thought you think.

As attention shifts, experience shifts. Change the relationship you have with your thoughts—and your experience of life will quietly begin to change with it.

Day 49 — When Obstacles Arise, Change Your Direction — Not Your Decision

Obstacles are not exceptions on the path to success—they are part of the path itself. No meaningful goal is ever achieved without resistance. Life does not test us by offering smooth roads; it tests us by asking whether we can continue when the road bends, narrows, or disappears for a while.

As the saying goes, *you can't change the direction of the wind, but you can adjust the set of your sails to reach your destination*. Life rarely moves in straight lines. Instead of stopping us outright, it interrupts us—forcing us to adapt.

Almost everyone knows this experience.

You are doing well. You are consistent. You have momentum.

You are exercising regularly, waking up early, eating better, staying organised, or steadily working toward a long-term dream. Then, without warning, life intervenes. Illness strikes. Work pressure increases. A family responsibility appears. There is loss, relocation, financial stress, or emotional upheaval.

Your routine breaks. Your rhythm is disturbed. Progress suddenly feels lost.

This moment often feels like failure—but it is not. Life getting in the way is not a personal flaw. It is reality.

The real test is not the obstacle itself. The real test is your response to it.

Some people interpret disruption as a signal to quit. They tell themselves, *"It's ruined now,"* or *"I'll start again someday."* Slowly, the goal is abandoned—not because it was impossible, but because flexibility was mistaken for weakness.

Others respond differently. They pause. They reassess. They adapt. They find another route forward. They continue—not in the same way, but with the same intention.

Obstacles do not cancel decisions. They demand adjustment.

When circumstances change, wisdom lies in changing the method, not the mission. The pace may slow, but the promise remains. If the gym is no longer possible, movement still is. If two hours of effort are no longer available, twenty minutes still count. If one strategy fails, another can be designed.

Progress does not disappear just because it looks different.

True determination is not rigid stubbornness. It is intelligent persistence. It is the ability to bend without breaking, to redirect without surrendering. Those who succeed are not the ones who avoid disruption—but the ones who refuse to let disruption decide the outcome.

Obstacles are detours, not dead ends.

When something blocks your path, do not question your purpose. Question your approach. Adjust your direction. Keep your decision intact.

Because success does not belong to those who never face obstacles—it belongs to those who keep going, even when they must go differently.

Day 50 — Be Like a Postage Stamp — Stick to One Thing Until You Get There

Most of us recognise this pattern in ourselves.

We decide to change something—our health, our habits, our work ethic, our routine. The intention is sincere. The beginning feels hopeful, even energising. And then, without drama or decision, we drift. A strict diet lasts a few hours before exceptions quietly slip in. A serious work plan loses momentum to distraction. A morning reading or meditation habit breaks on one rushed day and never quite finds its way back. A workout routine that once felt motivating slowly turns into "next week."

This doesn't happen because we are incapable. It happens because we don't stay long enough.

Success rarely fails due to lack of talent. It fails because attention is scattered before anything has time to grow.

A postage stamp is an ordinary object, almost forgettable. It doesn't rush. It doesn't change direction. It doesn't jump from place to place. It simply sticks—patiently and persistently—until the destination is reached. That is its entire power.

Life works the same way. You can achieve almost anything, but not everything at once. Those who move forward are not constantly chasing new ideas or fresh starts. They are the ones who finish what they begin before reaching for something new.

The problem is not ambition. The problem is distraction.

Human beings are restless by nature. New ideas excite us. Fresh beginnings feel light and full of promise. Meanwhile, unfinished goals feel heavy, uncomfortable, even dull. Instead of pushing through that discomfort, we escape into novelty. We jump from one intention to another, collecting beginnings but never reaching endings.

Digging ten shallow holes never brings water. Digging one deep well does.

When focus settles on one thing, something subtle but powerful happens. Mental noise softens. Energy gathers. Fear becomes easier to face. Learning deepens. Progress, though slow, becomes visible. The mind stops scattering itself and begins to move in one direction.

Our attention is limited. When it is divided endlessly, nothing receives enough nourishment to grow. Focus is not about doing more—it is about doing less, with care.

This does not mean shutting out the world forever. It means choosing one meaningful direction and committing to it long enough for something real to take shape.

Motivation will come and go. That is natural. What carries you forward is consistency. Showing up imperfectly still counts. Missing a day does not undo progress—abandoning the path does.

A postage stamp doesn't worry about speed. It only worries about staying attached.

Stay with the thing you chose when it feels boring. Stay when progress is slow. Stay when enthusiasm fades and doubt whispers. Because success is rarely built through dramatic effort. It is built through quiet persistence.

Be like a postage stamp. Stick to one thing—until you get there.

Day 51 - Agree to Disagree

At some point in life, we all discover an uncomfortable truth: not everyone sees the world the way we do.

People think differently. They believe differently. They choose differently. And no amount of explaining, arguing, or proving will always change that. Agreeing to disagree is not about surrendering your values or silencing your voice. It is about recognising that peace is often more valuable than being right.

Disagreements are inevitable. Conflict is optional.

Most arguments do not begin because people are evil or unreasonable. They begin because each person is deeply convinced that their view is correct. When both sides try to win, something else quietly loses—respect, connection, and sometimes the relationship itself.

Think of friendships strained by politics, families divided by beliefs, colleagues locked in endless debates. Often, the issue is not the difference of opinion, but the insistence that the other must see things the same way. When agreement becomes a condition for respect, relationships become fragile.

There is more than one way to see almost everything in life. Your perspective is shaped by your experiences, values, fears, and hopes—just as someone else's is shaped by theirs. Acknowledging this does not weaken your position. It strengthens your maturity.

Wisdom does not come from dominating conversations. It comes from understanding that truth is rarely owned by one side alone.

Agreeing to disagree is the quiet decision to let go of the need to convince. It is choosing to say, internally if not aloud, "I see that you think differently, and that is okay." You do not change your belief. They do not change theirs. The argument simply loses its grip.

This choice preserves energy. It protects peace. It allows relationships to breathe.

Emotional intelligence shows itself not in how loudly we defend our opinions, but in how calmly we handle opposition. When we stop taking disagreement as a personal attack, conversations soften. When we separate ideas from identity, respect survives even sharp differences.

You don't have to win every discussion. You don't have to have the last word. Some conversations are not meant to be resolved—they are meant to be released.

Agreeing to disagree is not weakness. It is restraint. It is confidence without aggression. It is knowing who you are well enough that you don't need universal agreement to feel secure.

Choose peace when possible. Choose understanding when available. Choose relationships over endless arguments.

Agree to disagree—not because your opinion doesn't matter, but because harmony often matters more.

Day 52 - Value the Process Over Result

There is a subtle misunderstanding that quietly misleads many people: the belief that the result is the reward. In reality, the result is only the visible end of a much deeper journey. The real reward is the person you become while walking toward it.

Training yourself to become capable of earning a million is far more valuable than possessing the million itself. Money can be lost. Circumstances can change. Success can disappear as quickly as it arrives. But the discipline, thinking, resilience, and self-trust built along the way do not vanish. Once earned, they stay with you. Knowing how to build something matters far more than simply having it.

When you commit to a process—when you keep going despite confusion, adapt instead of quitting, and learn instead of blaming—something important begins to shift inside you. At first, the change is invisible. Then it becomes undeniable. Your patience grows. Your confidence settles. Your reactions soften. You stop needing immediate proof because you trust the direction you're moving in. This inner transformation is quiet, but it is permanent.

Most people don't fail because they lack opportunity. They fail because they want the reward without becoming the person required to sustain it. They want success without responsibility, happiness without emotional strength, growth without discomfort. What arrives without inner preparation rarely stays. It collapses under its own weight.

Life, much like a long journey, reveals its lessons in stages. Each new level demands a stronger version of you. There is always a challenge guarding the next chapter—whether it is leadership, freedom, mastery, or peace. If you arrive without having gone through the process, the challenge does not move aside. It simply exposes what is missing.

This is why sudden success often feels hollow or destructive. Not because success is dangerous, but because growth was skipped. When change comes faster than character can keep up, old habits quietly reclaim control. Without the process, nothing new can last.

What we admire in people who succeed repeatedly is not just talent or timing. Beneath their visible outcomes lies an invisible structure built slowly—through consistency, discipline, and repeated effort. That structure was not created by chasing results. It was created by honoring the process, day after day, even when progress felt slow.

Even the simplest moments of life follow this truth. Nothing meaningful comes into existence fully formed. It unfolds. It requires steps, patience, and time. Skip the steps, and the outcome never appears. Respect them, and the result arrives naturally.

Results can disappear. Titles can fade. Money can be lost. But if you have gone through the process once, you can rebuild—often faster and wiser than before. The process teaches you not just how to win, but how to win again.

So place your attention where it belongs. Not on the finish line, but on who you are becoming as you walk toward it. When you take care of the process, the results no longer need to be chased.

They follow—quietly, inevitably, and in their own time.

Day 53 — The Happiness of Your Life Depends Upon the Quality of Your Thoughts

Just as the health of our body depends on the food we eat and the way we move, the health of our mind depends on the thoughts we repeatedly entertain. Thinking is not a neutral activity. It is a form of nutrition. Every thought feeds the mind, shaping how we experience life, how we feel, and how we respond to the world around us.

We often pay great attention to what we consume physically, yet remain careless about what we consume mentally. But the mind, just like the body, becomes what it is fed. When thoughts are nourishing, the inner world becomes calm and balanced. When thoughts are toxic, even the most comfortable life can feel heavy and restless.

What we focus on does not remain small—it grows. Attention is energy, and wherever that energy flows, expansion follows. When our focus stays fixed on things outside our control—other people's actions, past mistakes, imagined futures—we slowly give our power away. Life begins to feel overwhelming, not because it is, but because our attention is misplaced.

The mind is like a garden. Whatever we water grows. Weeds grow effortlessly; flowers require intention. Negative thoughts do not need encouragement—they arise naturally. Positive, peaceful thoughts must be cultivated deliberately. Left unattended, the garden of the mind fills itself with noise and clutter. Tended with care, it becomes a place of clarity and peace.

Life does not happen *to* us as much as it flows *through* us. Every experience passes through the filter of our thinking. Two people can live through the same moment and walk away with completely different emotional outcomes—not because life treated them differently, but because their thoughts interpreted the moment differently.

This is why peace begins not with changing the world, but with letting go of whatever competes with inner calm. Persistent negative emotions rarely come from circumstances alone; they almost always arise from repetitive negative thinking. Change the pattern of thought, and the emotional experience begins to change with it.

There is great freedom in realizing that while we may not control events, we always control our response to them. When this truth is understood deeply, life becomes lighter. A loss, a failure, or a setback may still hurt—but it no longer defines the entire experience.

Two people may lose the same job. One believes life is ruined. The other acknowledges the pain but sees a doorway opening. The event is identical. The experience is not. Happiness, therefore, is not a result of circumstances—it is a result of interpretation.

True satisfaction in life does not come from possessions, achievements, or approval. Those may bring comfort, but happiness comes from feeling at ease with oneself. It is an inner state, not an external reward. The mind is the home of happiness, and thoughts are its architects.

Thoughts are never empty. They carry emotional energy. That energy shapes behavior, words, and choices—and over time, it shapes life itself. If we want more peace, we must think peaceful thoughts. If we want gratitude, we must practise noticing what is already good. If we want a calmer tomorrow, we must choose gentler thoughts today.

A smile changes the world—not because the world changes, but because perception does. The same is true of thought. When thinking shifts, experience follows.

Happy people are not those with flawless lives. They are those who refuse to be imprisoned by circumstances. They do not hand over responsibility for happiness to people or outcomes.

Instead, they cultivate it quietly, internally, through awareness, acceptance, and conscious thought.

Happiness is not found. It is chosen—again and again, each day.

The happiness of your life truly depends upon the quality of your thoughts. Change your thinking—and your life will follow.

Day 54 — Make People Around You Feel Special

How you make people feel says far more about you than any title you carry, any position you hold, or any achievement you display. Long after roles fade and accomplishments are forgotten, what remains is the emotional imprint you leave on others.

Every human being wants the same few things at a deep level—to feel seen, valued, respected, and appreciated. This desire is universal. When someone consistently fails to make others feel good about themselves, it is often not a lack of manners or awareness, but a reflection of inner emptiness or unresolved insecurity.

Human beings are emotional first and logical second. We feel before we think. And then we use logic to justify how we feel.

Nothing in life is emotionally neutral. Every interaction leaves a trace—uplifting or draining, encouraging or diminishing. This is why we are naturally drawn toward people who make us feel lighter, stronger, and more confident about ourselves. We trust them without effort. We feel safe around them without explanation.

Making people feel special does not require money, authority, or grand gestures. It requires only presence and intention.

Sometimes it is as simple as a sincere compliment. Sometimes it is listening without interrupting. Sometimes it is remembering a name. Sometimes it is acknowledging someone who usually goes unnoticed.

A security guard who greets you by name. A colleague who listens fully instead of checking their phone. A senior who publicly appreciates effort, not just results.

These moments may appear small, but they carry immense emotional weight. A single gesture can change someone's entire day—and sometimes, their entire outlook.

A candle does not lose its light by lighting another candle. The room only grows brighter.

When you make people feel valued, doors begin to open—not because you are manipulating outcomes, but because you are practicing humanity. Respect, trust, and goodwill grow naturally around those who uplift others. People want to work with them, support them, and stand by them.

Everyone wants to feel like somebody. Nobody wants to feel invisible.

The person standing in front of you—regardless of status, role, or background—is just as important to themselves as you are to yourself. When this truth is understood, kindness becomes effortless.

Listening deeply. Speaking sincerely. Using names. Acknowledging effort. Noticing the quiet ones in the room.

These are simple acts, yet they hold extraordinary power.

Making others feel special does not diminish you—it elevates you. It reflects confidence, awareness, and inner strength. And in a world that often rushes past people without noticing them, being someone who truly sees others is a rare and beautiful gift.

Make people around you feel special. Because kindness costs nothing, yet returns everything.

Day 55 — Hard Work in the Right Direction Brings Results

Hard work matters—but hard work alone is no longer enough.

If effort by itself guaranteed success, then everyone who works long hours every day would already be successful. Yet reality tells a different story. Almost everyone at the top works hard—but so do most people at the bottom. This reveals an uncomfortable truth: hard work is necessary, but it is not the deciding factor.

The real difference lies in direction.

Many people confuse being busy with being productive. Days are filled with activity—emails, meetings, multitasking, constant motion—yet very little meaningful progress is made. Effort without direction creates exhaustion, not results.

Imagine two people pushing carts uphill. One pushes with all his strength, but the cart has square wheels. The other pushes with less effort, but the cart has round wheels.

Both are working hard. Only one is moving forward smoothly.

That is the difference between hard work and hard work in the right direction.

We see this clearly in everyday life. Take a student preparing for an exam. One studies for ten hours a day, memorizing everything mechanically, without understanding concepts or priorities. Another studies for fewer hours but with focus—understanding the syllabus, practising important questions, revising intelligently. The second student may work less, but the effort is aligned with the goal. That alignment makes all the difference.

This is the difference between efficiency and effectiveness.

You can become extremely efficient at doing things that don't really matter—and still remain stuck. Being efficient at the wrong task does not move you closer to success. Many people spend years working hard, only to realize they have been climbing fast on the wrong ladder.

Direction matters more than speed.

This is where the **80/20 principle** quietly operates in our lives. A small portion of our actions produces most of our results. A few skills, habits, or decisions create the majority of progress, while the rest consume time with little return. Successful people identify those high-impact actions and focus their energy there.

The most important question is not, *"Am I working hard?"* The real question is, *"Am I working on the right things?"*

Hard work without clarity is like driving fast without knowing the destination. Fuel burns, energy drains, and confusion grows. But when hard work is guided by clear goals, right priorities, smart strategies, and regular reflection, it becomes powerful—almost unstoppable.

Hard work is the engine. Direction is the steering wheel.

Without direction, hard work wears you down. With direction, hard work transforms you.

Don't just ask yourself whether you are working hard. Ask whether your hard work is taking you where you truly want to go.

Because hard work in the right direction always brings results.

Day 56 — Not the Years, but the Life in Your Years Counts

Life is not measured by how long you live, but by how well you live.

Every year, we celebrate birthdays and count candles. We mark age, but rarely pause to ask the more important question: *What did I do with those years?* A long life without meaning is not an achievement. A shorter life lived with purpose can echo far beyond its time.

Years do not define a life—impact does.

History reminds us of this truth again and again. Some people live eighty or ninety years and leave little behind except routines and regrets. Others live far fewer years and are remembered for generations because of what they stood for and how they lived. A life is remembered not by its length, but by its depth.

Life is like a book. Some books are thick but dull, filled with repetition. Others are short, yet powerful enough to change the reader forever.

Everyday life shows us the same contrast. One person lives on autopilot—wake up, work, eat, sleep, repeat. Days blur into years. Another lives with intention—learning, growing, facing fears, helping others, doing work that matters. Both age. But only one truly lives.

Time passes for everyone. The difference is how consciously we use it.

The real danger is not dying early—it is *just existing*. Many people don't live life; they endure it. They postpone living with promises like, "I'll enjoy life after retirement," or "I'll chase my dream once things settle," or "I'll be happy when circumstances change." But life does not wait. And by the time some people realize what truly matters, they are already running out of time—not because life was unfair, but because they were asleep to their own life.

This is why honest self-reflection matters. Do you wake up excited about your day? Do you enjoy what you are doing with your life? Are you growing, learning, evolving? Are you proud of the person you are becoming? If the answer is "not really," that is not failure—it is a wake-up call.

The beautiful truth is this: your life experience is yours to design.

Living a life that truly counts does not require fame, money, or perfection. It requires intention. It begins when you stop waiting and start choosing. When you decide to live consciously instead of drifting. When you take responsibility instead of complaining. When you act instead of postponing.

A meaningful life is built by living in alignment—with your values, your purpose, and your truth. It grows when you commit to learning, stay curious, and remain open to growth. A growing person feels alive. A stagnant one feels old—even at twenty-five.

Life becomes rich when you stop putting it on hold. There is no rehearsal. This is the performance. If you do not design your life, circumstances will do it for you. If you do not act on your dreams, they quietly fade—even the beautiful ones.

One day, your age will not matter. Your job title will not matter. Your bank balance will not matter. What will matter is how you lived. How you treated people. How bravely you followed your truth. How much life you brought into your years.

Don't aim to live long. Aim to live fully. Because in the end, it's not the years in your life that count— it's the life in your years.

Day 57 — Wake Up with Determination and Go to Bed with Satisfaction

Determination is the quiet force behind every meaningful achievement. Talent may help. Luck may assist. But without determination, nothing truly moves.

When you wake up each morning with a clear inner decision—*Today, I will give my best*—the tone of the entire day shifts. Your thoughts become focused. Your actions become intentional. Distractions lose their grip. Determination gives direction to energy that would otherwise scatter.

Determination is like the ignition of a car. The car may be expensive, well-built, and fully fueled—but unless the ignition is turned on, it goes nowhere. Determination doesn't guarantee a smooth road, but it guarantees movement. And movement, over time, changes everything.

When determination is present, discipline no longer feels like punishment. You stop forcing yourself and start choosing effort. A student who wakes up determined doesn't keep watching the clock. An athlete doesn't negotiate with excuses. A professional doesn't wait for motivation—they act first. Determination brings structure, and structure quietly produces results.

Life will present problems—daily, repeatedly, sometimes unfairly. Determination doesn't remove them, but it changes how you face them. A determined person doesn't ask, *Why is this happening to me?* They ask, *What is the next best move?*

Two people may face the same obstacle. One panics, complains, and mentally gives up. The other adjusts, communicates, adapts, and keeps moving forward. Same situation. Different determination.

Failure will visit everyone. It always does. But failure is not the opposite of success—quitting is. A determined person may fall many times, but they rise one more time than they fall. Failure does not weaken determination; it reveals it.

Think of a child learning to walk. The child falls again and again, yet never pauses to question whether walking is worth trying. That persistence is pure determination—untrained, instinctive, and powerful.

At the end of the day, satisfaction does not come from doing everything. It comes from doing what mattered. You may not complete every task. You may not win every battle. But if you stayed honest with your effort, focused on what was important, and acted in alignment with your values, you sleep peacefully.

Satisfaction is the quiet voice at night that says, *I showed up today.*

But determination, strong as it is, is not endless. If health, relationships, and mental peace are neglected, it slowly burns out. Just like a phone battery—no matter how powerful the device, without recharging, it shuts down. Caring for yourself is not selfish; it is strategic. Eat well. Move your body. Rest deeply. Spend time with people who energize you.

A simple rhythm makes life powerful:

Wake up with determination—decide who you want to be today. Move through the day with focus—do what needs to be done, not what feels easiest. Go to bed with satisfaction—knowing you honored your effort.

When lived consistently, days turn into progress, and progress turns into purpose.

Wake up with determination. Go to bed with satisfaction. Repeat—until success becomes inevitable.

Day 58 — Learn to Ignore What Does Not Matter

Every moment of our lives, thoughts rush into our minds—one after another, endlessly. Most of them are unnecessary, distracting, or completely irrelevant. When we try to give attention to everything, we don't become informed or aware—we become overwhelmed, exhausted, and unfocused.

Think of a student sitting in a classroom. What truly matters in that moment is listening, understanding, and learning. Yet the mind often drifts—to who is sitting where, what someone is wearing, what happened earlier, or what might happen later. None of these thoughts help the student learn. They only steal attention.

Life works the same way.

Every day, countless things compete for our attention—opinions, gossip, noise, news, criticism, comparisons, and trivial events. Most of them add no real value to our lives. In fact, nearly ninety percent of what distracts us is irrelevant. If we don't learn to ignore it, we slowly lose clarity, peace, and productivity.

Imagine your mind as a phone battery. Every useless thought, argument, or distraction drains it. If you waste your battery on meaningless apps, there's nothing left when you actually need power. Attention is limited. Where you spend it decides how you live.

A powerful question to pause and ask yourself is: **"Will this matter in two years?"**

If the answer is no, it probably doesn't deserve your emotional energy today.

Ask yourself another, deeper question: **"If I had only one year**

left to live, would I spend it worrying about this?"

Would you spend that year endlessly scrolling, reacting, arguing, or consuming noise? Or would you invest it in learning, relationships, health, growth, and meaningful work?

Time is the most valuable thing you own—and the easiest to waste. At some point, many of us start behaving as if time is unlimited. It isn't.

Many people live in constant reaction mode—responding to every comment, criticism, opinion, or provocation. But reacting to everything means being controlled by everything. Maturity is knowing what deserves a response—and what deserves silence.

There is a simple truth:

Weak people seek revenge.

Strong people choose forgiveness.

Intelligent people learn to ignore.

Ignoring is not weakness. It is wisdom. It is the discipline to protect your mind from noise and reserve your energy for what truly matters.

Learn to ignore what does not help you grow. Learn to ignore what steals your peace.

When you do, life becomes lighter, clearer, and far more meaningful.

Day 59 — Show Up, No Matter What

There is a quiet truth behind almost every success story: most of it comes down to simply showing up.

We often romanticize success. We imagine breakthroughs, lucky moments, dramatic wins. But long before any of that happens, there is something far less glamorous—presence. Turning up. Being there. Again and again.

You may not always control outcomes, results, or timing. But you can always control one thing: whether you show up.

And showing up changes everything.

When you show up, you put yourself in motion. You may not see progress immediately, but something is always happening beneath the surface. You are learning. You are adjusting. You are becoming. Showing up is the causal mechanism of success—the one action that always comes first. Before results, before confidence, before clarity, there is presence.

Life, much like a game, has a simple rule: if you don't show up, you're out. Not because you lost—but because you never gave yourself a chance to win. Dreams don't fail us; absence does. Goals don't disappear; we walk away from them.

What makes showing up difficult isn't effort—it's fear. Fear of failure. Fear of judgment. Fear of rejection. These fears convince many people to stay away, to wait, to delay. And by staying away, they quietly forfeit their future. Showing up takes courage precisely because it exposes you to uncertainty. But that same exposure is what allows growth to happen.

The most important thing about showing up is this: it shapes who you become.

Be the person who stayed. Be the person who tried again. Be the person who didn't disappear when things got uncomfortable.

Progress is rarely visible in the beginning. This is where most people get confused—and quit. They go to the gym for months and see no change. They study consistently and feel like nothing is sticking. They work hard without immediate recognition. It feels pointless. Invisible. Discouraging.

But this invisible phase is where success is actually being built.

Think of bamboo. For years, nothing appears above the ground. But underneath, strong roots are forming. When growth finally comes, it happens rapidly. Those who stop early never see it. Those who keep showing up do.

The people who succeed are not always the most talented or the luckiest. They are simply the ones who stayed in the game longer than everyone else.

Showing up means honoring your commitments—even when motivation disappears. Motivation is emotional and unpredictable. Discipline is quiet and reliable. Discipline shows up daily.

Show up when it's exciting. Show up when it's boring. Show up when it's uncomfortable. Show up when you feel stuck.

Because every time you show up, you keep the door open. And as long as you are still showing up, success is still possible.

Show up—no matter what.

Day 60 — The Only Impossible Journey Is the One You Never Begin

Ask yourself honestly: what is really stopping you from getting what you want?

Most of the time, it isn't lack of ability, resources, or intelligence. It isn't even the difficulty of the journey. What truly stops us is the fear of the first step.

The unknown feels threatening. Failure feels embarrassing. Judgment feels heavy. And so, instead of admitting fear, we disguise it as logic. We tell ourselves comforting stories: *I'll start when the time is right. I need more preparation. I'm not ready yet.* These excuses feel safe. They protect us from discomfort.

But comfort zones are dangerous places. Nothing grows there.

Many people spend their lives waiting for the perfect moment—perfect conditions, perfect confidence, perfect clarity. The problem is simple: that moment never arrives. Life will always be messy. Responsibilities will always exist. Fear will never fully disappear. Time, however, keeps moving forward—whether you move with it or not.

Learning to swim offers a simple truth. No one learns by standing at the edge of the pool forever, reading instructions and watching others. At some point, you must step into the water. The first splash is uncomfortable. The first moment feels awkward. But that discomfort is the price of progress.

Growth always begins at the edge of comfort.

Every meaningful change starts with a difficult first step—the first workout, the first honest conversation, the first attempt after failure, the first decision to try again. That step rarely feels confident. It feels uncertain. But once it is taken, clarity begins to appear. You don't need to see the entire staircase. You only need to take the next step. The rest reveals itself as you move.

Nature understands this better than we do.

Mother eagles build their nests high on cliffs. Their eaglets are protected, fed, and safe. But when the time comes to fly, the mother does something that appears cruel—she pushes the eaglet out of the nest. The fall is terrifying. Panic sets in. And then something extraordinary happens. Wings stretch. Muscles awaken. Instinct takes over. The eaglet flies.

The fall was not punishment. It was preparation.

Many of us remain in our own nests—staying in jobs we dislike, delaying dreams, avoiding risks, choosing comfort over growth. Not because we are incapable, but because we haven't jumped. Fear keeps asking, *What if you fall?* What it never tells you is this: you cannot discover your wings without leaving the nest.

So ask yourself one honest question: *Do I believe in myself—even a little?*

If the answer is yes, begin. Not tomorrow. Not someday. Now.

You don't need certainty. You don't need perfection. You only need the courage to start.

Because the truth is simple: the thrill of soaring always begins with the fear of falling. And the only journey that truly fails is the one that never begins.

Begin. The path unfolds only for those who take the first step.

Day 61 — Be Brave Enough to Be Bad at Something New

Have you ever wanted to try something new but stopped yourself because you feared looking foolish? Have you ever watched someone excel—on a stage, on a field, or in a profession—and quietly told yourself, *"I could never do that"*?

What we often forget is a simple and humbling truth: every expert was once a beginner.

The people we admire today did not begin with confidence, clarity, or mastery. They began with uncertainty. They stumbled. They struggled. They failed repeatedly. No athlete starts on a podium. No speaker begins with a flawless voice. No artist creates brilliance on the first attempt. What separates them from the rest is not talent alone—it is courage. The courage to start badly, and the patience to stay long enough to improve.

Think about learning to ride a bicycle. No one glides effortlessly on the first day. We wobble, fall, scrape our knees, and feel embarrassed. Yet we do not give up cycling for life because of a few falls. We get back up. We try again. And slowly, without even noticing when it happens, balance replaces fear. What once felt impossible becomes natural.

Every skill follows this same pattern—public speaking, writing, swimming, coding, leadership, fitness, even relationships. The beginning is always uncomfortable. The middle is often frustrating. But mastery belongs to those who remain.

Being bad at something is not failure. It is proof that you are learning. Growth requires uncertainty. Waiting until you feel confident is a trap, because confidence is not a prerequisite—it is a result. You do not feel ready and then act. You act, and readiness follows.

Visit any gym and you will see this truth clearly. The beginner often feels awkward, comparing themselves to those who appear strong and disciplined. But every fit body there was once unfamiliar with the equipment, sore after simple exercises, and filled with doubt. The difference is not confidence on day one—it is consistency despite discomfort.

Growth lives outside comfort. Change feels threatening because it disrupts what is familiar. But staying comfortable costs more than trying and failing ever will.

Be willing to look clumsy. Be willing to make mistakes. Be willing to learn in public.

Take the leap even when your voice shakes and your steps feel unsure. The version of you that succeeds is not found in waiting—it is shaped through starting.

You do not become good before you begin. You become good because you begin—and stay.

Being brave enough to be bad at something new is not weakness. It is the first, essential step toward becoming great.

Day 62 — Trust the Timing of Your Life

Everything in life happens for a reason. Every person who enters your life, every chance encounter, every experience, every conversation, and even the smallest moment—pleasant or painful—carries meaning.

Nothing is random. Each obstacle you face and every opportunity you receive is part of a larger design, quietly guiding you to where you need to be. Sometimes the purpose is obvious. Often, it is not. Many lessons reveal their meaning only with time. That is why learning to trust the timing of your life is essential.

Every individual moves according to a different inner clock. Some reach milestones early. Others arrive later. Neither path is superior, and neither is a failure. They are simply different journeys. Comparison distorts perspective. What looks like delay is often preparation in disguise.

When life becomes difficult, the mind naturally asks, *"Why is this happening to me?"* But years later, when you look back, you begin to see how those very moments shaped you—building maturity, resilience, patience, and wisdom that you could not have developed any other way.

As Steve Jobs once said, you cannot connect the dots looking forward; you can only connect them looking backward. That is why trust is required. The challenges and opportunities you face today are preparing you for something you cannot yet see.

Moving slowly does not mean you are stuck. Growth is not always visible. Sometimes life slows you down because it is strengthening your foundation. Relax. You will find your path. You will build your career. You will form the right relationships. You will become who you are meant to be—when the time is right.

Trusting the timing of your life does not mean doing nothing. It does not mean leaving everything to fate. Trust means showing up fully in the present—doing your best today without being consumed by anxiety about tomorrow. Work sincerely. Focus on the process. Let outcomes unfold in their own time.

Not everything will happen the way you imagine—and that is okay. No one gets everything in life. Acceptance brings peace. Everything you have lived through has prepared you for this moment.

You are not late. You are not early. You are exactly where you need to be.

Trust the timing of your life.

Day 63 — There Is Less Traffic Beyond That Extra Mile

Going the extra mile means doing what most people are unwilling to do. It is the quiet choice of effort over comfort, humility over ego, and excellence over adequacy. It is not merely about correcting what went wrong, but about delivering something better than what was expected.

Most people stop at what is required. They meet expectations, do the minimum necessary, and wait for results. Very few go beyond that line—and that is precisely why the extra mile remains uncrowded. There is less traffic there because fewer people are willing to walk it.

The principle is simple: life rewards those who give more than they are asked to give. When you consistently offer more value than what you are paid for, praised for, or expected to deliver, compensation eventually follows—often in forms you did not anticipate. This is not instant, but it is inevitable.

Standing out is surprisingly simple, though not easy. Because most people do only what is necessary, small actions create a big difference. Showing up prepared, following through, paying attention to details, and adding value without being asked immediately sets you apart. Excellence is not complicated—it is just uncommon.

People often say, "It's lonely at the top." That loneliness exists because very few are willing to walk far enough to reach it. The extra mile demands effort when no one is watching, persistence without immediate reward, and responsibility without recognition. As effort increases, crowds thin out.

Going the extra mile is not a one-time decision—it is a habit. It begins quietly in small places: in your current role, in how you handle responsibility, in how you treat people, and in how seriously you take your work. Over time, this habit expands your capacity and attracts opportunities that average effort never reaches.

The moment you decide to think differently, act differently, and deliver more than expected, you will notice something powerful. The road ahead becomes quieter. The competition fades. The path opens up.

There is less traffic beyond the extra mile.

And that is exactly where growth, opportunity, and success are waiting.

Day 64 — Success Is How High You Bounce When You Hit Bottom

Success is often misunderstood. We tend to admire people when everything is going right—when they are winning, progressing, and being applauded. But those moments reveal very little about real strength. Anyone can look confident when life is smooth. True success is revealed when life collapses and you are forced to respond.

Every meaningful journey includes failure. Plans fall apart, dreams crack, confidence fades, and sometimes life pushes us all the way to the bottom. These moments feel final, almost unbearable, but they are rarely the end. More often, they are interruptions—necessary pauses meant to realign us with a deeper version of ourselves.

Failure has a way of stripping away illusion. It humbles the ego and exposes what truly matters. It forces reflection and asks uncomfortable questions: *What went wrong? What must change? Who must I become now?* In this way, failure becomes a teacher—harsh, honest, and transformative.

Those who rise are not the ones who never fall. They are the ones who refuse to remain where they have fallen. They observe, learn, and move forward with greater awareness and discipline. This is why failure often carries more wisdom than success ever can. Success can inflate the ego, but failure sharpens the mind.

Rock bottom holds an unexpected gift. When nothing is left to lose, fear weakens its grip. Clarity emerges. Courage returns quietly, without noise. From that place, rebuilding becomes possible—not with arrogance, but with resilience.

Life does not ask us to avoid falling. It asks us to rise with understanding. You may not control the cards you are dealt, but you always control how you play them. Strength is not found in perfection—it is found in recovery.

Success isn't about avoiding the fall. It's about how powerfully—and how wisely—you rise.

Day 65 — Always Dream Big

Every meaningful achievement begins long before results appear. It begins as a dream—quiet, invisible, often dismissed by others, and sometimes doubted even by the dreamer. If you want a dream to come true, you must first allow yourself to have one.

Every self-made achiever—whether a business leader, an athlete, an artist, or a reformer—started with a dream at a time when there was no proof it could work. Dreams act like a compass. Consciously or unconsciously, we move in the direction of our dominant inner images. When those images are small, life remains small. When they are large, life begins to expand.

The moment you allow yourself to dream big, something subtle yet powerful shifts within you. Your self-esteem rises. You begin to respect yourself more—not because you have achieved anything yet, but because you are no longer thinking at the level of limitation. Confidence grows quietly when you aim higher.

Think of a child flying a kite. If the child grips the string too tightly out of fear, the kite never rises. But when the child allows it to climb into the open sky—even if it trembles in the wind—the kite reaches heights impossible near the ground. Dreams work the same way. When you loosen your fear and allow your aspirations to rise, growth becomes possible.

Ordinary people often dream only what feels safe or realistic. That is why their lives remain confined to familiar boundaries. Extraordinary people dare to dream beyond their current ability—and then grow into those dreams. Dreams stretch belief systems. They quietly challenge old assumptions: *Maybe I can learn more. Maybe I can try again. Maybe I am capable of more than I thought.*

History offers powerful reminders of this truth. At a time when independence seemed impossible, Mahatma Gandhi held onto a vision that many mocked and dismissed. His dream did not change the world overnight. It changed him first. And through that inner transformation, an entire nation followed.

Big dreams function like a gym for the soul. At first, the weight feels overwhelming. But with time and effort, strength develops. Challenges appear not to defeat you, but to prepare you. Slowly, you become the kind of person capable of carrying larger responsibilities.

Dreaming big also expands your world. New skills emerge. New people enter your life. New environments challenge you. What once felt distant slowly becomes familiar.

You do not dream big because you are powerful. You become powerful because you dared to dream big.

Never underestimate what you are capable of becoming. Your dreams are not accidents—they are invitations, calling you toward a greater version of yourself.

Day 66 — Make Your Foundation Strong

If you want to build a tall skyscraper, you must first build a deep and solid foundation. No matter how impressive a structure looks from the outside, if the base is weak, collapse is only a matter of time. Life follows the same law. The bigger your dreams, the stronger your foundation must be.

We admire the finished skyscraper, but we rarely think about the years spent digging deep into the ground, pouring concrete, reinforcing steel, and repeating the same slow, unglamorous work. In life, we want the height—success, recognition, money, fitness—but we resist the process that makes it possible. This is why stories of "overnight success" are so appealing. They suggest that results can come without preparation. But hope does not build foundations. Discipline does.

Consider someone who suddenly wins the lottery. For a brief period, life feels extraordinary. Yet most lottery winners lose everything within a few years. The reason is simple: they received the result without building the foundation—financial discipline, emotional control, patience, and responsibility. The same pattern appears in fitness. Crash diets and extreme routines may give quick results, but without habits, consistency, and care, the weight returns—often stronger than before.

Foundations are built slowly. They require repetition, patience, and a willingness to do small, boring things when no one is watching and no progress is visible. Just as buildings rise floor by floor, success is built habit by habit.

Most people don't fail because they lack talent or desire. They fail because their foundation is weak. Motivation carries them for a few days, then disappears. Without systems, routines, and structure, progress collapses the moment life becomes uncomfortable. Discipline remains when motivation fades.

A strong foundation rests on order, routine, and health. When your environment is chaotic, your mind struggles to focus. When your days lack structure, you rely on willpower—and willpower always runs out. When your body is neglected, your energy collapses, taking ambition with it. No dream survives exhaustion.

Strengthening your foundation does not require dramatic changes. It requires consistency. A stable morning routine. Clear daily and weekly intentions. Regular movement. Better food choices. Quality sleep. Periodic self-reflection. Reduced distractions. None of these actions are glamorous. All of them are essential.

Your foundation is not built once and forgotten. Life creates cracks. Habits slip. Energy fluctuates. What matters is awareness. Just as engineers inspect buildings for weakness, you must regularly examine your routines, health, and discipline—and repair what is weakening.

Everyone wants a skyscraper life. Very few are willing to dig deep enough to support it.

If you want success that lasts, stop chasing shortcuts. Build your foundation patiently—floor by floor, habit by habit. Because when the foundation is strong, nothing can shake what you build on top of it.

Day 67 — Self-Doubt Is the Only Barrier

"When you doubt your power, you give power to your doubt."
— Honoré de Balzac

You know that voice.

The one that whispers, *"You can't do this." "You're not good enough." "You'll fail again."*

It appears the moment you decide to grow. It grows louder when the path becomes uncomfortable. And when you fall, it doesn't help you stand—it questions whether you should have tried at all.

That voice is self-doubt.

Self-doubt is subtle and persistent. It doesn't always shout; sometimes it simply hesitates for you. It drains confidence quietly, clouds judgment slowly, and steals momentum without asking permission. And the most dangerous moment is not when doubt appears—but when you believe it.

Because the moment you believe self-doubt, you hand over your power.

Most people try to fight doubt with forced positivity. They repeat affirmations, deny fear, or pretend confidence. But doubt doesn't disappear through resistance. The harder you fight it, the stronger it pushes back.

Self-doubt is like a shadow. You cannot eliminate it by attacking it. You learn to move forward while it follows.

Like fear, sadness, or uncertainty, doubt is part of being human. The goal is not to eliminate it—but to understand it and stop letting it decide your actions.

Think of self-doubt like a smoke alarm. Sometimes it signals something useful—a lack of preparation, a skill to improve, a blind spot to address. Other times, it goes off for no real reason at all. If you smash the alarm, you lose awareness. If you panic every time it rings, you never move. Wisdom lies in listening, evaluating, and responding calmly.

One of the most powerful shifts you can make is learning to reframe your inner dialogue. When the mind says, *"I can't do this,"* pause and add one word: *yet.* When it asks, *"What if I fail?"* gently ask back, *"What if I learn?"*

This small change turns doubt from a stop sign into a signal.

Self-doubt is also strengthened by the voices you allow around you. Some people call themselves "realists," but what they offer is often fear disguised as advice. People who have abandoned their own dreams often try to make others feel foolish for having theirs. Protect your mental environment. Choose voices that encourage effort, not avoidance.

When doubt feels overwhelming, return to evidence. Self-doubt has selective memory—it forgets every challenge you survived. Remind yourself of problems you once thought unbearable and overcame anyway. If you have done hard things before, you are capable of doing hard things again.

Above all, learn to be kind to yourself. You will live your entire life in your own company. If that relationship is built on constant criticism, every journey becomes exhausting. Treat yourself with patience. Encourage yourself the way you would encourage someone you care about deeply.

Self-doubt never fully disappears. It shows up whenever you step outside comfort, aim higher, or attempt something meaningful. That is not weakness—it is growth. Doubt becomes dangerous only when it replaces action.

Confidence is not the absence of doubt. Confidence is movement in its presence.

Every time you act despite doubt, it loses authority. Every step forward strengthens trust in yourself.

Self-doubt is not the enemy—inaction is. Listen to doubt, learn from it, but never let it decide your future. The moment you choose action over hesitation, you take your power back.

Day 68 — Every Winner Was Once a Loser

Every teacher was once a student. Every expert was once a beginner. And every winner—without exception—was once a loser.

Success does not begin with talent, luck, or intelligence. It begins with learning. No one is born accomplished. The people we admire today reached where they are by walking through failure, rejection, embarrassment, and defeat. What separates them from the rest is not that they avoided loss—but that they refused to let loss define them.

Failure, for them, was never a verdict. It was feedback.

They did not stop when things went wrong. They paused, adjusted, learned, and tried again.

Success and failure are not permanent labels. They are temporary positions on a moving journey. Where you stand today does not determine where you will stand tomorrow—unless you decide that it does.

Think of learning to ride a bicycle. Everyone falls. Some fall once, feel the sting, and declare, *"I'm bad at this."* Others fall, get back up, shift their balance slightly, and try again. The difference is not ability. It is persistence. And persistence is simply learning in action.

History quietly confirms this truth again and again.

Thomas Edison was told by his teacher that he was "too stupid to learn anything." He went on to invent the electric bulb—after thousands of failed attempts. He never called them failures. He called them discoveries of what didn't work.

Walt Disney was fired for "lacking imagination." Soichiro Honda was rejected by Toyota. Vincent van Gogh sold almost nothing during his lifetime. Steven Spielberg was rejected multiple times by film school. Albert Einstein was considered slow as a child.

None of these people began as winners. They became winners because they stayed students.

Failure is not proof that you are incapable. It is proof that you are in motion.

Every rejection adds resilience. Every mistake builds experience. Every loss, if examined honestly, sharpens wisdom. The people who succeed are not those who never fall—they are those who refuse to stop learning how to rise.

If you feel like a loser today, pause and look again. You may not be losing at all.

You may be learning.

Every winner was once a loser who refused to quit. Stay in the game. Keep learning. Your story is still unfolding—and the best chapters are often written after the hardest lessons.

Day 69 — Prioritize Your Health

When asked whether health should be a priority, almost everyone agrees without hesitation. Yet, when we observe how life is actually lived, our actions often tell a very different story.

Work deadlines pile up. Family responsibilities demand attention. Social obligations fill the calendar. Celebrations, routines, and endless to-do lists consume our days. Somewhere along the way, health quietly slips to the bottom—postponed for "later," when things slow down. We know what to do: eat better, move more, sleep well, drink water, manage stress. But knowing has never been the problem. Doing is.

The most common excuse is also the most convincing one: *"I'm too busy."* But the truth is uncomfortable—we are not too busy. We are simply prioritizing other things over our health. When something truly matters, we find the time, just as we find the money for what we value. Health works the same way.

People who succeed in maintaining good health do not have fewer responsibilities. They make one conscious decision: they prioritize themselves. This is not selfishness. It is self-respect. You cannot pour water from an empty glass. A body that is exhausted and neglected cannot support a meaningful career, strong relationships, or a peaceful mind. Taking care of yourself is not abandoning others—it is ensuring you can show up fully for them.

Health does not happen accidentally. It is created intentionally. Exercise enters life because it is scheduled. Good nutrition happens because meals are planned. Rest becomes possible because bedtime is protected. Mental peace grows when space is created for stillness. Motivation may start the journey, but organization and consistency sustain it.

Anyone can eat well for a day or exercise for a week. The real challenge is not starting—it is continuing. Discipline must replace motivation, because motivation fades, but habits endure.

Every healthy choice is an investment. Like money, good investments compound over time, while poor ones create future liabilities. Junk food, inactivity, chronic stress, and poor sleep may feel convenient today, but they demand heavy payment tomorrow.

Most of today's major illnesses—heart disease, diabetes, stroke, cancer—are not sudden accidents. They are often the result of years of lifestyle choices. The most hopeful truth is that many of these conditions are preventable. Genetics may load the gun, but lifestyle pulls the trigger.

Health is the foundation beneath everything else. Without it, success cannot be sustained. Energy, focus, patience, resilience, and emotional balance all depend on how well you care for your body and mind. Mental health is not separate from physical health; the two are deeply connected. What you repeatedly think eventually shows up in how you feel and function.

Self-respect begins with self-care. Health is not about appearance or numbers on a scale. It is about the quality of your daily life—how you wake up, move, think, and engage with the world.

Your health is not something to focus on after success, responsibilities, or achievements. It is the foundation that makes all of them possible. When you prioritize your health, you are not losing time—you are gaining life.

Day 70 — Build Trust, Build Success

Trust is the invisible foundation beneath every successful relationship—whether in leadership, family, friendship, or the workplace. Skills may impress, systems may scale, and authority may command compliance, but without trust, none of it lasts. Relationships might continue on the surface, yet underneath, they slowly weaken. And eventually, they break.

Simply put, success without trust is temporary.

Trust is never built in a crowd. It is built quietly, one person at a time. A leader does not earn trust from "the team" through a single speech or meeting. Trust grows through individual interactions—through consistency, presence, and behavior repeated over time. It is formed in everyday moments: how promises are kept, how people are treated, and how decisions are explained.

Trust cannot be bought. Titles, money, and power may create compliance, but they do not create belief. As the Dalai Lama once said, trust cannot be purchased in a supermarket. People trust only when they feel genuinely valued—not as resources, followers, or means to an end, but as human beings.

We understand trust most clearly when it disappears. When trust is broken, people rarely announce it. Instead, they withdraw. Engagement fades. Energy drops. People still show up physically, but mentally they step back. They stop contributing ideas, stop caring deeply, and stop going beyond the minimum. It is a quiet disengagement—an internal strike that often goes unnoticed until it is too late.

At its core, trust means feeling safe while being vulnerable. Any relationship—personal or professional—requires vulnerability. Trust eases the anxiety that vulnerability brings. When trust is present, communication flows naturally. When it is absent, every interaction feels fragile and guarded.

Low-trust environments shrink effort. People give only what feels necessary, not what they are capable of. High-trust environments, on the other hand, inspire loyalty, honesty, and discretionary effort. People give more—not because they are forced to, but because they want to.

The danger of lost trust is that it is rarely discussed openly. Most people do not say, "I no longer trust you." They simply pull away. Ironically, repairing trust requires a minimum level of trust to begin the conversation. When that moment passes, distance grows silently.

Trust is slow to build and easy to destroy. And once broken, it cannot be rushed back. Many choose to walk away rather than risk being hurt again. This is why trust must be handled with care—protected deliberately, not assumed casually.

Trust grows where reliability exists—where words are followed by action. It deepens with transparency, when information is shared openly and people are not left guessing. It strengthens when competence supports good intentions, and when sincerity aligns words, values, and behavior. Fairness, genuine listening, and respect sustain it. And perhaps most importantly, trust flourishes where vulnerability is allowed—where people can admit mistakes, say "I was wrong," and remain human without fear.

Trust is fragile, invisible, and priceless. It takes time to earn, moments to lose, and great effort to rebuild. If you want lasting success—in leadership, relationships, or life—guard trust as your most valuable asset. Because when trust grows, people grow with it.

Day 71 — You Have a Unique Identity

Each individual is unique—because there is no one else exactly like you. Comparison only makes sense in a world where everyone is the same. But life was never designed that way. Even identical twins grow into different people, shaped by their thoughts, emotions, choices, and experiences. When we compare ourselves with others, we are measuring one unique journey against another—and that is where unnecessary frustration begins.

Everyone lives life differently. We think differently. We speak differently. We learn, believe, dream, and grow in our own way. What excites one person may leave another untouched. What feels meaningful to you may feel irrelevant to someone else. That is not a flaw in life's design—it *is* the design.

You are the driver of your life, not a passenger. So why exhaust yourself trying to keep pace with trends you don't believe in, or chasing a version of success that doesn't resonate with you? Why copy someone else's life when your own carries untapped potential? If someone doesn't like you for who you are, that does not mean you need to change—it simply means you are not meant to live for their approval.

Many people lose themselves trying to fit in. They adjust their personality, silence their instincts, and hide their true nature just to feel accepted. Over time, this performance becomes exhausting—and sometimes irreversible. Authenticity is not weakness. It is courage. It takes strength to stand as you are in a world that constantly pressures you to conform.

You were born with something only you have. Your way of seeing the world. Your interpretation of experiences. Your emotional responses. Your inner questions and insights. No one else thinks exactly like you. No one else feels life the way you do. That perspective is not accidental—it is essential.

You create your own life experience through the meaning you give events, the choices you make, and the way you respond to success, failure, joy, and pain. Even when two people face the same situation, their inner experience is never the same. That is uniqueness in action.

Differences are natural, not problems. As we grow, we begin to understand that not everyone will like what we like, want what we want, or believe what we believe. When we accept this, life becomes lighter. Judgment softens. Peace grows. Everyone is special—just in different ways.

Society often tries to standardize uniqueness. It tells us how to look, what to chase, how to measure success, and what happiness should resemble. But real confidence does not come from fitting in. It comes from standing comfortably in who you are—even when that looks different.

There will always be someone who appears "better" by certain measures—more successful, more admired, more talented in a particular area. That is simply reality. But comparison ignores a deeper truth: everyone carries value in different forms. Some lead. Some listen. Some create. Some heal. Some think deeply. Some quietly support others. Your strength may not look like someone else's—but that does not make it smaller.

You are not meant to be a copy. You are meant to be one of a kind.

Your uniqueness is not a flaw—it is your strength. The moment you stop trying to be like others, you begin to become fully yourself. And that is where real confidence, peace, and purpose begin.

Day 72 — Grow Gradually

Growth is always gradual. It rarely announces itself. It happens quietly, through the small choices we make every single day.

Every decision—what you eat, how you speak to yourself, how you respond under pressure, whether you show up or give up—moves you slightly in one direction or another. Over time, these tiny movements shape the kind of person you become.

We do not suddenly become better or worse overnight. We become better or worse one decision at a time.

We all want results—and we want them fast. There is nothing wrong with achieving something quickly. But trouble begins when we become obsessed with speed and begin to ignore the process. This constant urgency slowly drains our health, our happiness, and our peace.

The world celebrates outcomes, not effort. We are shown success, wealth, recognition, and victory—but rarely the discipline, patience, and repetition behind them. This creates the illusion that results define our worth, when in reality, it is the journey that shapes our character.

Fast success can feel exciting. Slow growth is transforming.

When growth is gradual, something deeper happens. You don't just achieve—you evolve. You become someone stronger, more grounded, more dependable. Someone whose values are stable, whose confidence is earned, and whose standards rise naturally.

Achievements can fade. Character stays.

Rome was not built in a day. But bricks were laid every hour.

Rome is the result. The bricks were the system.

Goals tell you where you want to go. Systems determine whether you actually get there.

Laying one brick does not feel impressive. It doesn't attract applause. It doesn't feel heroic.

But laying one brick every day—consistently, patiently, without drama—is how lasting success is built.

You don't need to build everything today. You don't need to have life completely figured out. You only need to ask one simple question:

What is the next small brick I can lay today?

One disciplined choice. One honest effort. One good habit repeated. That is how real growth happens.

Growth is not loud.It is not instant. It is not glamorous. But it is powerful.

Stay committed to small daily improvements, and time will do what motivation cannot. Just keep laying bricks.

Day 73 — Be a People's Person

People are the most valuable resource you will ever have. Your success, fulfillment, and happiness are deeply influenced by how well you relate to others. No matter how intelligent, skilled, or hardworking you are, progress in life rarely happens alone. It moves through conversations, cooperation, trust, and connection.

To live well—and to lead effortlessly—you must learn not just how to manage tasks, but how to understand people.

Some individuals walk into a room and instantly shift the atmosphere. They don't dominate conversations or seek attention. Yet people feel comfortable around them. Drawn to them. Seen by them. Their power lies not in what they say, but in how they make others feel.

Leadership expert John Maxwell captured this truth simply: people do business with people they like—and even when logic suggests otherwise, they still do.

Being a people's person does not mean being loud, fake, or overly outgoing. It means being genuinely interested in people—not for what they can offer you, but for who they are. It means creating emotional safety. Acceptance. Warmth. Presence.

Science supports this. Human brains are social. They synchronize. Emotions are contagious. When someone enters a space calm and positive, others begin to mirror that state. When someone enters anxious or negative, the same happens. People don't just listen to your words—they feel your inner state.

True influence does not come from authority. It comes from character. People don't follow titles—they follow authenticity.

A person who can put others at ease, make them smile, and help them feel valued carries a rare and powerful skill—one that strengthens relationships, careers, and communities alike.

At its core, being a people's person is simple: You listen. You help without keeping score. You take interest in what matters to others. You leave people feeling lighter than when you found them.

Every human being carries the same quiet emotional needs—to be appreciated, respected, and valued. When you meet these needs in others, resistance dissolves and cooperation grows naturally.

People skills are life skills. No matter how competent you are, your ability to work *with* people determines how far you go. Charm, when genuine, is not manipulation—it is emotional intelligence in action. It is the art of making someone feel important in your presence.

At the deepest level, every person wants the same thing: to feel that they matter.

Being a people's person is not about impressing others. It's about connecting with them.

If you learn to value people, understand them, and uplift them, you will never lack support, opportunity, or fulfillment. Because when you win people, you win life.

Day 74 — There Is No Competition, Only You

A flower does not compete with the flower next to it. It simply blooms.

That single image holds a profound truth about life. You are not here to defeat others, outshine them, or race ahead of them. You are here to become yourself—fully, honestly, and steadily.

As Bill Gates once said, he is not in competition with anyone but himself. His only goal is continuous improvement. This mindset frees you from comparison and places responsibility exactly where it belongs—within.

When you compete with others, bitterness quietly enters. Someone always seems ahead. Someone always appears to have more—more success, more recognition, more progress. Comparison turns life into a scoreboard you never asked to play on. But when you compete only with your past self, something changes. Growth begins. Peace follows.

Life may look like a race, but it isn't. It is a journey toward your own unrealized potential. Your only real opponent is the version of you that refuses to grow.

Everyone is playing a different game. Different strengths. Different timelines. Different paths.

Judging yourself by someone else's standards is like judging a fish by its ability to climb a tree. Comparison ignores context and creates false conclusions. And in a world of constant screens and highlights, it has become dangerously easy to measure your behind-the-scenes against someone else's best moments.

When you stop competing with others, freedom appears. You no longer panic when someone succeeds before you. You no longer feel threatened by progress that isn't yours. You trust your own timing.

As Iyanla Vanzant wisely said, comparing yourself to others is an act of violence against your authentic self.

Competing with others never truly works. There will always be someone better. Winning by someone else's metrics does not guarantee growth. And comparison, once practiced daily, becomes a habit that erodes gratitude and confidence.

Self-competition, on the other hand, creates real winners.

When you compete with yourself, success is no longer about beating someone—it's about giving your best effort, staying true to your values, and growing consistently. The process matters more than the podium.

Success begins to look different: mastering a skill, building discipline, becoming emotionally stronger, thinking more clearly.

This kind of success is deeply fulfilling because the reward is internal. There is no need to boast. And when one milestone is reached, you don't stop—you grow again, not to prove anything, but because growth itself has become the goal.

Your authentic self has no competition. No one thinks exactly like you. No one experiences life exactly as you do. No one expresses the world through your lens.

The moment you stop fighting for identity and start embracing who you truly are, pressure dissolves and peace takes its place.

You are not losing in life. You are only distracted by other people's paths.

Step out of comparison. Stop standing in borrowed shadows. Remember your own light.

There is no competition— there is only you, becoming more of who you were meant to be.

Day 75 — Criticism Is Important

If you always believe you are right—and never seek feedback—how do you truly know whether what you are doing is effective, meaningful, or even useful?

Honest feedback works like a mirror. It reflects what you cannot see on your own—your blind spots, your rough edges, and the areas where growth is still possible. Without that mirror, improvement becomes guesswork. You may move forward, but not necessarily in the right direction.

Criticism, when understood correctly, is not an attack. It is information.

Criticism is often misunderstood. It is not trolling, insults, or abusive commentary. Those are noise and deserve no attention. Real criticism is constructive, specific, and actionable. It points to something concrete and offers the possibility of improvement.

Compliments make you feel good. Criticism makes you better.

This is why growth slows when criticism disappears. Without honest negative feedback, weaknesses remain hidden. Mistakes repeat themselves. Opportunities quietly slip away. Over time, this doesn't just limit progress—it creates avoidable failure.

History offers many reminders of this truth. When feedback is ignored early, consequences arrive later—often at a much higher cost. Early criticism may feel uncomfortable, but it prevents future embarrassment and regret.

Criticism serves several important purposes.

First, it keeps you humble and grounded. It forces you to examine your work honestly instead of protecting your ego. When you learn to separate criticism from identity, you gain the ability to correct faults early rather than defending them stubbornly. Criticism is not a verdict on who you are—it is feedback on what you did.

Second, criticism expands your thinking. A critic offers a different lens, a viewpoint you may never have considered. For those with fragile self-esteem, criticism feels threatening. For those with maturity, it becomes a gateway to insight. A sincere critic is far more valuable than a flattering supporter—because flattery keeps you comfortable, while criticism pushes you forward.

Third, criticism tests and builds your people skills. How you respond matters as much as what is said. A defensive or angry reaction turns small criticism into lasting conflict. A calm, respectful response often disarms the critic and earns respect from observers. Over time, handling criticism well sharpens emotional intelligence—a skill that quietly determines how far you rise.

Criticism also gives you a chance to practice forgiveness. Harsh words naturally trigger the urge to retaliate or hold a grudge. But resentment harms the holder, not the speaker. The critic moves on. You carry the weight. Letting go is not weakness—it is emotional strength.

Criticism will never feel pleasant. But it is one of life's most honest teachers.

Those who avoid criticism remain average. Those who learn from it grow stronger, wiser, and more capable.

Don't fear criticism. Listen carefully. Respond wisely. Use it selectively.

What challenges your ego today may sharpen your character tomorrow.

Day 76 — Investment in Knowledge Pays the Best Interest

Every successful person in the world shares one quiet habit. They invest in learning—consistently, intentionally, and daily. They read. They observe. They ask questions. They remain curious long after formal education ends.

Knowledge is not something they collect for display. It is something they use to think better, decide better, and live better.

Among all forms of wealth, knowledge is the only one that cannot be taken away. Money can be lost. Positions can change. Fame can fade. But what you place in your mind stays with you for life. Once acquired, knowledge does not diminish—it compounds. Each new insight strengthens the next, creating depth, clarity, and confidence over time.

Knowledge is more than power. It is freedom.

It frees you from blind decisions. It frees you from dependence on guesswork. It frees you to see possibilities where others see limitations. Without knowledge, choices are based on assumptions. With knowledge, decisions are rooted in understanding.

In today's fast-changing world, learning is no longer optional. It is a survival skill. Tools evolve. Industries shift. Skills expire. Those who stop learning are not left behind because they lack ability—but because they stop adapting. Curiosity keeps you relevant. Learning keeps you resilient.

Everything you know today was once unfamiliar. Every skill you possess was once a mystery. The difference between average and exceptional people is not intelligence—it is intentional learning.

Knowledge creates opportunity. And opportunity creates

income, confidence, and independence. The more you learn, the more valuable you become—not just to employers or markets, but to yourself. Faster learning often leads to faster earning, but more importantly, it leads to better living.

If you want the highest return on your time, effort, and money, invest in yourself. Material investments fluctuate. Self-investment compounds for life. What you learn today continues to serve you tomorrow—and for years beyond.

Knowledge also sharpens judgment. When facts are clear, decisions become strategic instead of risky. Understanding turns uncertainty into confidence. This is why learning quietly improves every area of life—career, relationships, leadership, and self-respect.

Many people say they are too busy to learn. In reality, learning is not what steals time—it is what saves it. Those who make time to learn make fewer costly mistakes, move faster with clarity, and adapt sooner than others.

Life, in many ways, resembles a game of chess. The better you understand the rules, patterns, and strategies, the less likely you are to lose. Knowledge doesn't guarantee success—but ignorance almost guarantees struggle.

Knowledge is the foundation of growth, opportunity, and confidence. The more you know, the more capable you become. And the more capable you become, the richer your life grows—inside and out.

Invest in knowledge. It pays the best interest—for a lifetime.

Day 77 — Do Not Care What Others Think

Much of our mental energy is wasted living inside other people's heads. We imagine their opinions. We judge ourselves through their eyes. We carry the weight of thoughts that were never ours to begin with.

Here is a truth that is both simple and freeing: **Other people's opinions of you are none of your business.**

What others think of you is shaped by their past, their beliefs, their fears, their expectations, and their unresolved issues. Their opinions say far more about *them* than they ever say about *you*.

No matter who you are or what you do, you cannot win everyone. Some people will like you without effort. Some people will dislike you without reason. And most people will not think about you at all.

This has nothing to do with your worth. It is simply human nature.

Yet many people live their entire lives trying to manage perceptions—editing themselves, shrinking their truth, filtering their choices—just to avoid imagined judgment. In doing so, they slowly stop living for themselves and begin living for approval.

The fear of opinions runs deep because it is ancient. Thousands of years ago, belonging to a group meant survival. Rejection meant danger. That wiring still exists in the human brain, even though the threat no longer does. Today, disapproval rarely costs us our lives—but it still costs us our freedom.

The exhausting part is this: you are worrying about something you cannot control.

People will interpret your words, your silence, your success, your failure, your clothes, your confidence, your hesitation—each in their own way. One person may admire you. Another may misunderstand you. A third may judge you unfairly.

And there is nothing you can do about it.

Your responsibility is not to manage opinions. Your responsibility is to live with integrity.

Self-respect is the real shield. When you respect yourself, outside voices lose authority. External validation may feel good, but internal validation is what brings peace. When you know who you are, noise becomes background static.

There is also a liberating realization most people miss: People are far more focused on themselves than on you.

Everyone is busy managing their own worries, insecurities, and ambitions. The spotlight you feel is often imagined. The judgment you fear is usually fleeting—or nonexistent.

Caring too much about opinions comes at a high cost. Your personality tightens. Your choices become cautious. Your life starts revolving around expectations instead of values.

Letting go is not an instant switch—it is a practice. Each time you notice yourself seeking approval, you gently return to what matters to *you*. Over time, this practice creates space. And that space feels like freedom.

You were not born to be approved by everyone. You were born to be yourself.

The moment you stop carrying other people's opinions, you begin carrying your own life. And that is where clarity, courage, and peace quietly begin.

Day 78 — Be Ready to Face Rejection

Rejection is not a detour in life. It is part of the road.

Everyone encounters it—regardless of talent, preparation, intelligence, or effort. Rejection does not mean you are incapable. It does not mean you are unworthy. It simply means you tried to move forward.

And that matters.

Rejection does not define who you are. **Your response to it does.**

If you want meaningful success—big or small—you must be willing to hear "no" before you hear "yes." There is no ambition so modest that it avoids rejection, and no dream so bold that it reaches fulfillment without it.

Rejection hurts. That truth cannot be romanticized away. Reading books, watching videos, or repeating affirmations does not make rejection painless. But pain is not the problem. Resistance is.

You cannot avoid rejection. But you can choose how you meet it.

When rejection is met with grace instead of bitterness, something powerful happens. You gain clarity. You gain resilience. You gain direction. Instead of shrinking, you expand. Instead of quitting, you adjust.

Seen clearly, rejection is not an ending—it is feedback.

It shows you what needs improvement, where growth is required, or whether a different direction might serve you better. The setback itself is neutral. Meaning is created by how you interpret it.

There is a comforting myth that successful people are somehow protected from rejection. They are not. Every person you admire has faced doors slammed shut, opportunities denied, and moments of deep discouragement.

The difference is simple: They did not stop.

Falling down happens to everyone. Staying down is a decision.

Often, rejection is not removal—it is redirection. What feels like loss in the moment frequently reveals itself as alignment in hindsight. Doors close so that better ones can open. Paths end so that stronger ones can begin.

History is full of reminders. People rejected for being "unfit," "unskilled," or "unimaginative" went on to reshape industries, culture, and thought. Their rejection did not weaken them—it refined them.

Rejection becomes more frequent as you challenge yourself more. That is not a flaw—it is a sign of growth. Comfort zones protect ego but starve potential. Stepping forward invites resistance, and resistance builds strength.

Each "no" moves you closer to the right "yes." Each rejection teaches you how to stand taller the next time.

Those who succeed are not the ones who avoid rejection. They are the ones who recover from it quickly and move forward wisely.

You are not failing when you are rejected. You are participating.

Rejection is proof that you are in motion, not standing still. And those who keep moving—learning, adjusting, and continuing—eventually arrive.

Face rejection. Learn from it. And keep going.

Day 79 — Expand Your Comfort Zone

A comfort zone is a psychological space where life feels familiar, safe, and predictable. It is where routines are known, habits are established, and anxiety stays low. Inside it, you feel in control. You know what to expect—and how to respond.

There is nothing wrong with this space. We all need moments of stability, rest, and calm.

The problem begins only when we refuse to leave it.

Comfort itself is not the enemy. **Stagnation is.**

When life becomes too comfortable, growth quietly slows down. Challenges are avoided. Goals are postponed. Opportunities pass unnoticed. Over time, what once felt like safety begins to feel like limitation. Comfort slowly turns into a cage—not because it is harmful, but because it is incomplete.

Growth lives outside what feels safe.

New skills, confidence, strength, and self-belief are not built in familiar territory. They are forged in uncertainty—where outcomes are unclear and effort feels awkward. As Neale Donald Walsch observed, life truly begins at the edge of the comfort zone.

Inside comfort, life is smooth. Outside it, life is formative.

Smooth waters do not create strong sailors. Skill is developed not by avoiding storms, but by learning to navigate them. The same is true for human growth. Confidence is not born from certainty—it is earned through exposure to uncertainty.

Most of our daily life happens within comfort. We know how to manage responsibilities, follow routines, and meet expectations. Familiarity keeps anxiety low, even when life is demanding. That is why comfort feels so attractive.

But when you step just beyond it, something changes.

There is a moment—a small tightening in the chest, a hesitation in the mind. A quiet thought appears: *What if I fail? What if I look foolish?* That feeling is not a warning to retreat. It is a signal that growth is near.

Fear, like a muscle, weakens with use.

The first time you do something new, fear feels intense. The second time, it softens. The third time, it fades further. Each exposure strengthens you. Each survival expands your sense of capability.

Imagine your comfort zone as a fenced boundary. The first time you step beyond it, the shock is sharp. But each time you cross, the boundary loses power. Eventually, what once frightened you becomes familiar. The comfort zone does not disappear—it expands.

And that expansion reinforces itself.

The more you step outside what feels safe, the more capable you feel. The more capable you feel, the easier the next step becomes. What once felt intimidating slowly becomes ordinary.

You don't need to make dramatic leaps. You only need to step slightly beyond what feels safe—again and again.

Growth does not happen in comfort. But comfort grows when you are brave enough to expand it.

Step out. Feel the twinge. Grow stronger.

Day 80 — Own Your Morning

Someone once said, *"Show me a person's morning routine, and I'll tell you who they are."* That statement carries more truth than it appears to at first glance.

How you begin your morning is not just about time management—it is about identity. It reveals your priorities, your discipline, and the direction in which your life is moving. In many ways, your morning routine is a preview of your future.

Your morning sets the tone for your entire day—and eventually, for your life.

A focused window of just thirty minutes to one hour in the morning can transform your clarity, productivity, and emotional balance. This is not accidental. It is intentional. Highly successful people, across industries and cultures, take their mornings seriously—not because they have more time, but because they understand leverage.

When you own the morning, you reduce the chaos that follows.

Your morning routine becomes an anchor. No matter how difficult yesterday was, no matter how demanding today looks, the morning remains your constant. It is your protected space—time that belongs only to you. In that space, you reconnect with yourself before the world starts making demands.

As life becomes busier, this ritual becomes even more essential. Without it, you begin the day reacting. With it, you begin the day responding.

There is no universal formula for the perfect morning. The most effective routine is not the one copied from someone else, but the one that works for *you*. It should align with your lifestyle, energize your body, steady your mind, and prepare you emotionally for the day ahead.

Ask yourself honestly: Do you wake up because you *have to*—and rush into the day half-present? Or do you wake up with intention—and create a meaningful start?

When you begin the day by nurturing your physical energy, calming your thoughts, and grounding your emotions, something powerful happens. You step into a peak state. And peak states create peak performance. You are less reactive, more focused, and better equipped to handle whatever comes your way.

Winning the day does not require controlling everything. It requires controlling the beginning.

You don't need to fix your entire life overnight. You only need to own your morning.

When you own your morning, you own your day. And when you own your days, you quietly elevate your life.

Start tomorrow morning—on purpose.

Day 81 — You Only Fail When You Give Up

Making your mark on the world is hard. If it were easy, everyone would do it.

Success demands patience, commitment, and resilience—and it almost always comes with failure along the way. The real test is not whether you avoid failure, because you won't. Failure is not the opposite of success. It is part of the journey toward it.

Every person who has ever achieved something meaningful has passed through failure. Often repeatedly. There are no shortcuts. In fact, winners usually fail more times than others—the difference is that they stay in the game long enough to learn.

Failure is not the end of the road. It is the road.

There are phases in life when nothing seems to work. Effort feels wasted. Results refuse to show up. Rejections pile up, one after another. In those moments, it's easy to believe you have failed. But the truth is quieter and far more hopeful: you haven't failed—you just haven't succeeded *yet*.

Trying one method and failing doesn't mean the goal is impossible. It only means that approach didn't work. The biggest mistake people make is not failing—it's quitting too early.

History is full of people who looked like failures until they didn't quit. Early setbacks, rejection, financial collapse, public embarrassment—none of these stopped them. What would have happened if even one of them had decided, *This is it. I'm done*? The world would be poorer for it.

The difference between winners and quitters is not talent, intelligence, or luck. It is persistence.

Winners stay with the task. Quitters leave when discomfort begins.

As long as you are trying, learning, adjusting, and moving forward, you are not a failure. Failure, when faced honestly, builds strength. It sharpens judgment. It stretches capacity. It toughens the spirit. What breaks some people becomes the training ground for others.

You fail only at one moment in life—when you stop trying completely.

As long as you keep showing up, you are still in the game. And if you are still in the game, success is still possible.

There is a powerful real-life reminder of this truth in the story of **Chandeep Singh Sudan** from Jammu & Kashmir. As a young athlete, he competed in football and skating at high levels. Then, in 2011, a tragic accident changed everything. An electric shock of 11,000 volts left him with fourth-degree burns. To save his life, doctors had to amputate both his arms.

For most people, that would have been the end of the story.

For him, it became a turning point.

Skating without arms is unimaginably difficult. Balance depends on them. He fell again and again. Progress was slow and painful. But quitting was never an option. Through relentless effort, he learned to skate again—without what the world said he needed.

Today, he is a national-level skater, a world-record holder in para skating, an international medalist in Taekwondo, an engineer, and a civil services aspirant. His journey proves a simple truth: adversity does not decide your outcome—your response does.

Failure does not define you. Giving up does.

As long as you keep trying, adjusting, and moving forward, you have not failed.

Stay in the game. Keep showing up.

Because success belongs to those who refuse to quit.

Day 82 — Always Expect the Unexpected

To expect the unexpected does not mean becoming pessimistic or fearful. It means becoming mentally prepared.

It means holding two truths at the same time: hoping for the best while being ready for disruption. You stay grounded rather than shocked. Alert rather than anxious. Flexible rather than rigid.

Life rarely unfolds the way we imagine.

We make plans with confidence, believing that effort guarantees outcomes and intentions ensure stability. Yet again and again, life reminds us otherwise. You plan an outdoor celebration—and it rains. You plan a lifelong marriage—and separation happens. You plan for a dream college or career—and the door closes. You plan to remain healthy—and illness appears without warning.

This is not failure. This is life being life.

Much of what happens around us lies beyond our control. The world is constantly changing—sometimes dramatically, sometimes quietly, but always unpredictably. We want fairness. We want logic. We want life to reward good intentions consistently. When it doesn't, disappointment follows.

But disappointment does not mean life is cruel. It means life is uncertain.

And within that uncertainty lies opportunity.

Every disappointment carries something hidden: a lesson, a redirection, a chance to adapt, or a reason to grow stronger. Life may not always give you what you want—but it often gives you what you need next. Sometimes you welcome what arrives. Sometimes you resist it. Either way, life moves forward, and so must you.

Some days feel light and effortless. Other days feel heavy and draining.

Both are necessary.

Together, they shape your resilience, your wisdom, and your character. What matters is not the kind of day you receive, but how you respond to it. Calm acceptance on hard days is just as important as gratitude on good ones.

The only certainty in life is uncertainty.

No matter who you are—rich or poor, powerful or ordinary, confident or confused—the future remains unknown. Tomorrow may bring joy. Tomorrow may bring pain. More often than not, it brings a mix of both.

And the biggest changes in life rarely send advance notice.

Paths you believed in may suddenly close. Plans you worked toward may need to be abandoned. Change often arrives uninvited, disrupting comfort and certainty. Yet many of life's most meaningful transformations begin in moments we never planned for.

This is why adaptability matters more than control.

You cannot manage everything that happens to you. But you can choose how you respond. The ability to adjust your expectations, rethink your direction, and remain emotionally steady is one of the most powerful strengths a person can develop. Change may unsettle you at first—but over time, it often leads you somewhere better.

Life will surprise you—sometimes gently, sometimes painfully.

Don't resist it. Don't fear it.

Expect the unexpected. Stay flexible. Stay hopeful.

Because when you accept uncertainty, you gain resilience—and resilience is what carries you forward through whatever comes next.

Day 83 — Free Is Usually Expensive

Free things are tempting. They feel light, effortless, and risk-free.

A platform like social media appears free—and undeniably useful. But beneath that convenience lies an uncomfortable truth: free is rarely free. If you're not paying with money, you are paying with something else—your time, your attention, your energy, your privacy, or the opportunities you never pursue because you were distracted.

And those costs are often far more expensive than money.

Everything in life has a price. If something doesn't charge you cash, it charges you invisibly. Time spent scrolling, focus fragmented, attention hijacked, or energy drained—these payments are quiet, but they accumulate. The real question is not whether something is free. The real question is what currency you are paying with.

This is why "free advice" is often the most dangerous. Advice that costs nothing is rarely examined deeply. People accept it casually, apply it loosely, and later pay the price through wrong decisions or wasted years. Advice without accountability feels safe—but safety without results is costly.

We live in a world overflowing with free offers. Free apps. Free trials. Free content. Free tools. At first glance, it feels like abundance. But step back and you'll see a simple truth at work: nothing is truly free. Someone always pays. And often, that someone is you.

The biggest hidden cost of free is time.

Time is the one resource you can never earn back. A free product that wastes hours can cost more than a paid one that saves minutes. Before clicking "free," few people pause to ask what they are giving up instead—learning, creating, resting, building, or simply being present.

Free often comes with invisible trades. Your privacy is exchanged quietly, one form at a time. Your data is collected, analyzed, and stored for years. You receive a short-term benefit; someone else receives long-term access to you. Your attention becomes the product. Platforms are designed not to serve you—but to keep you engaged for as long as possible.

There is also a psychological cost. When something is free, it is rarely valued. Commitment stays low. Action remains shallow. Distraction rises. When you pay—even a small amount—you show up differently. You pay attention. You engage. You take responsibility. Payment creates intention. Free often creates noise.

This does not mean free is always bad. It means free should never be accepted blindly.

Pause before accepting what costs nothing. Ask yourself what you are really paying with—and whether the exchange serves your long-term growth or quietly drains it.

Free is not the enemy. Unexamined free is.

Before you accept something free, ask what it will cost you in time, focus, and direction. Because in the long run, the most expensive choices are often the ones that looked free at the beginning.

Day 84 — You Are the Architect of Your Destiny

You are not a passenger in your life. You are the architect.

Destiny is often spoken of as something mysterious—something written in advance, waiting to unfold. But destiny is not a matter of chance. It is a matter of choice. Every decision you make today, no matter how small it appears, is shaping the life you will live tomorrow.

No one can think for you. No one can work for you. No one can dream for you. And no one can turn those dreams into reality on your behalf.

That responsibility—and that power—belongs to you alone.

Your future is not something you discover one day. It is something you create every day. Destiny does not arrive suddenly or dramatically. It is built quietly, through habits, attitudes, and repeated actions. What you do consistently matters far more than what you intend occasionally.

Every choice carries weight. How you spend your time. How you respond to setbacks. How you treat people when no one is watching. How you handle failure, disappointment, and uncertainty.

These choices may feel ordinary in the moment, but together they form the architecture of your life. Over time, they compound. What feels insignificant today becomes decisive tomorrow.

Success, then, is never an accident. Those who build meaningful lives do not rely on luck or fate. They plan, they work, they adjust, and they persist. When plans fail, they redesign. When progress slows, they reinforce the foundation. Destiny does not carry them forward—they carry themselves.

At some point, every person must confront a simple truth: if your present life is shaped by your past actions, then your future life will be shaped by what you choose next. Responsibility is not a burden—it is freedom. Because the moment you take responsibility, you reclaim power. The power to change. The power to improve. The power to rebuild.

You may not control everything that happens to you. But you always control how you respond. And response, repeated over time, becomes direction.

You do not wait for destiny. You do not hope for destiny. You build it.

Brick by brick. Choice by choice. Action by action. Pick up the tools. Draw the blueprint. And begin—because your life is under construction, and you are the architect.

Day 85 — Changing Your Attitude Changes Your Altitude

Your attitude is your window to the world.

It is the mental lens through which you interpret life. Two people can stand in the same place, face the same situation, and yet experience two completely different realities—because their attitudes are different. One sees possibility. The other sees limitation. The circumstances do not change. The perspective does.

This is why attitude matters more than conditions.

A problem seen as a burden remains heavy. The same problem seen as a lesson becomes lighter. Failure viewed as an end stops movement. Failure viewed as a stepping stone creates momentum.

Life does not respond to events alone—it responds to interpretation.

Rain falls on everyone. Obstacles visit everyone. Discomfort touches every life. What separates people is not what happens, but how they rise in response. Some stay grounded in complaint. Others lift themselves above the clouds.

You always have more choice than you think.

Attitude is not something that happens to you—it is something you choose. You choose how you look at life, how you interpret setbacks, how you respond to people, and how you speak to yourself in quiet moments. Your attitude is shaped by your thoughts—and your thoughts are yours to direct.

In this sense, you are not only living your life—you are designing your mind.

What you focus on expands. What you magnify gains power. What you ignore slowly fades. When your thinking improves, your emotional state shifts. When emotions stabilize, actions become wiser. And when actions improve, results naturally rise.

This is why consistently successful people think differently. Their minds are not overcrowded with negativity, cynicism, or constant complaint. They maintain mental clarity. They look for solutions instead of excuses. They learn instead of resent. They adapt instead of resist.

A negative attitude is rarely bad luck. More often, it is poor mental discipline.

Just as the body requires training, the mind requires conditioning. When you train your thoughts, your attitude strengthens. And when your attitude strengthens, your altitude increases—quietly, steadily, and sustainably.

You don't rise in life by changing everything around you. You rise by changing what happens within you.

Change your attitude. And your life will naturally rise to meet it.

Life will challenge you—but attitude determines how far you rise.

You may not control every situation, but you always control how you see it and how you respond.

Change your attitude. And you will change your altitude— in life, work, and personal growth.

Day 86 — The Real Taste of Success Comes After Failure

Success tastes different when you have failed before. It is richer, deeper, and more meaningful—because you understand what it cost to reach there. When you have experienced disappointment, rejection, and self-doubt, success no longer feels accidental. It feels earned.

Just like food without salt feels bland, success without struggle often feels empty. It may look impressive from the outside, but it lacks depth on the inside. Failure adds texture to success. It gives it weight, value, and perspective.

When things come easily, we rarely pause to appreciate them. But when success follows long periods of effort, uncertainty, and persistence, it stays with us. Think of water after hours of thirst. Think of rest after exhaustion. The relief, gratitude, and satisfaction are incomparable. That is what success feels like after failure.

Failure has an unfair reputation. It is treated as something shameful—something to hide or escape from. Many people abandon their dreams not because they lack ability, but because they are afraid of failing along the way. Yet failure does not mean you are incapable. It simply means that something did not work this time.

Failure forces reflection. It slows you down and asks you to look closely—at your approach, your preparation, your mindset. It teaches you what books cannot. In that sense, failure is not a verdict. It is guidance. It redirects effort, sharpens focus, and quietly builds resilience.

Endurance is the unseen ingredient behind meaningful success. Continuing when progress is slow. Showing up when motivation fades. Standing again after being knocked down.

This endurance shapes character—and character is what gives success its lasting satisfaction.

Often, the hardest phase appears just before the breakthrough. The struggle sharpens your hunger. The pain deepens your gratitude. And when success finally arrives, it feels real—not borrowed, not fragile.

Failure is not the opposite of success. It is part of the recipe.

If you are struggling right now, it does not mean you are losing. It may simply mean you are being prepared. Because the real taste of success is known only by those who have failed, endured, and refused to give up.

Day 87 — Learn to Prioritize

When everything feels important, nothing truly gets the attention it deserves. Work expands. Responsibilities multiply. Commitments pull from every direction. And before you realize it, the day ends with movement—but very little progress.

This is not a time problem. It is a priority problem.

Life becomes overwhelming when we treat all tasks as equal. Prioritization is how you regain control—not by doing more, but by choosing better.

Being busy is easy. Being effective is not. Prioritization turns effort into results and noise into clarity.

At the heart of prioritization is a simple distinction. Some things are important. Some things are urgent. And many things are neither. Important tasks shape your future. They align with your values, long-term goals, health, relationships, and growth. They matter deeply—but they rarely shout for attention. Urgent tasks demand immediate action. They push you into reaction mode. Some are necessary. Many are simply loud.

The danger is living only in urgency. When you constantly react, you feel productive—but you slowly drift away from what truly matters.

The most meaningful progress happens when you deliberately make time for what is important but not urgent: planning, learning, relationships, self-care, and long-term thinking. These are the quiet builders of a good life. They don't pressure you—but they shape you.

Equally important is learning what not to do. Not every message needs a response. Not every request deserves a yes. Some tasks can be delegated. Others can be ignored altogether. Time spent on low-value activities quietly steals energy from high-impact work.

One simple practice can change everything. At the end of each day, decide what truly matters tomorrow. Not everything—just a few important tasks. Rank them. And the next day, begin with the most difficult and meaningful one. When the hardest task is done, the rest of the day feels lighter. Momentum replaces stress.

Prioritization is not about perfection. It is about intention. It is the daily decision to protect what matters most from what matters least.

You don't need more time. You need clearer choices.

Doing everything is exhausting. Doing the right things is powerful.

Let priorities—not pressure—decide your day.

Day 88 — Set a Mission for Yourself

Just as organizations need a mission to guide their decisions, individuals need one too. Without a mission, it is easy to drift—busy, occupied, and exhausted, yet unsure why. A mission gives direction when choices feel overwhelming and clarity when life gets noisy. It answers a quiet but powerful question: *Why am I doing what I'm doing?*

A personal mission statement is not about success as the world defines it. It is about meaning as *you* define it. It reflects your values, your beliefs, and the kind of person you are committed to becoming. When you have a mission, decisions become simpler. You may still face difficulty, but you are no longer confused about direction.

Life inevitably brings phases of doubt—moments when confidence dips, progress slows, or comparison creeps in. During such times, goals alone are not enough. Goals can change. Circumstances can shift. Motivation can fade. A mission, however, remains steady. It acts like a compass, gently pulling you back to what truly matters.

Creating a mission does not require complex language. It begins with honest reflection. What do you stand for? What kind of life feels meaningful to you? What values are non-negotiable? When these answers come together, they form a simple statement—clear, personal, and grounding. It becomes something you return to when life feels scattered.

A mission does not limit you; it frees you. It helps you say no to distractions and yes to the right struggles. It aligns your actions with your inner values. And when effort feels heavy, it reminds you why the effort is worth it.

A personal mission is not something you write once and forget. It evolves as you evolve.

But having one keeps you from drifting. It gives your life direction, even on uncertain days.

Set your mission. Live by it. Return to it when the world gets loud.

Because when you know *why* you are here, you stop wandering—and start living with intention.

Day 89 — Overthinking Pauses Everything

Overthinking has a quiet way of stopping life without making any noise. From the outside, nothing seems wrong. But inside, the mind keeps moving—replaying moments, predicting outcomes, questioning decisions that haven't even been made yet. You are not resting, yet you are not moving forward either. You are paused.

At its heart, overthinking is not depth—it is overload. The mind lingers too long on the same thought, hoping that one more round of analysis will bring certainty or relief. Instead, it brings fatigue. The more you think, the heavier everything feels.

Overthinking often begins with anxiety. Anxiety tries to protect you by preparing for every possible scenario. But the mind was never meant to carry the future all at once. When preparation turns into rumination, thinking loses its usefulness and becomes a burden.

What makes overthinking deceptive is that it feels like responsibility. It feels like problem-solving. But most of the time, it produces no clarity—only delay. No action follows. No decision is made. Life waits while the mind keeps circling the same question.

Trying to force thoughts to stop rarely helps. The mind resists pressure. What softens overthinking is gentle awareness—pausing long enough to notice that not every thought is true, and not every thought requires a response. Some thoughts are simply mental noise passing through.

Overthinking pulls you away from the only place where life actually happens—the present. When the mind lives in the past, regret grows. When it rushes into the future, fear takes over. And in both cases, the moment where movement is possible is missed.

Clarity does not arrive through mental force. It arrives through calm attention.

You don't need to think more to move forward. You need to trust yourself enough to stop thinking in circles.

When the mind settles, direction appears. And when overthinking releases its grip, life quietly begins to move again.

Day 90 — Don't Try to Copy — You Are Unique

Each one of us enters the world carrying something that has never existed before—and will never exist again. There has never been another you, and there never will be. That alone makes you irreplaceable.

Yet, somewhere along the way, many of us forget this truth. We begin to watch others closely—how they speak, how they live, how they succeed—and slowly, almost unconsciously, we start measuring ourselves against them. We imitate what looks admired. We adjust who we are to fit in. And without realizing it, we begin drifting away from ourselves.

You do not need everyone's approval to live a meaningful life. Some people will understand you. Some will not. That has nothing to do with your worth. Trying to reshape yourself to be accepted by everyone is exhausting work—and it never leads to peace. Peace arrives only when you stop asking for permission to be who you are.

Nature never copies itself. No two leaves are the same. No two sunsets are identical. A flower does not look at the flower beside it and wonder if it should bloom differently. It simply blooms. Quietly. Fully. In its own time.

Copying others often comes from a hidden belief that who you are is not enough. But perfection does not exist. What you call flaws are often the very traits that give you depth, originality, and humanity. When you try to become someone else, you don't improve—you dilute what is already powerful within you.

You are unrepeatable. Your thoughts, emotions, experiences, and perspectives form a combination that has never existed before. No one sees the world through your eyes. No one feels life exactly the way you do. That uniqueness is not an accident—it is your contribution.

Fulfillment does not come from imitation. It comes from alignment. From listening inward instead of outward. From allowing yourself to grow into who you truly are, rather than shrinking yourself to match someone else's shape.

You were not created to be a copy. You were created to be an original.

The moment you stop trying to resemble others, you begin discovering your own strength.

Be yourself—fully, honestly, and without apology. That is where confidence begins, and where your real life quietly unfolds.

Day 91 — Nobody Can Hurt You Without Your Permission

There is a quiet truth most of us discover only after many emotional battles: pain does not come from events alone—it comes from the meaning we attach to them.

You always have a choice. A choice about what you focus on. A choice about what you believe. A choice about how deeply you let something enter you.

Two people can face the same words, the same criticism, the same rejection—and walk away feeling entirely different. One carries wounds for years. The other shrugs and moves on. The difference is not strength or sensitivity. The difference is interpretation.

The moment you realize that your reactions are not automatic, but chosen, something shifts inside you. You begin to pause instead of react. You observe your thoughts instead of obeying them. Slowly, consciously, responses replace reflexes. And over time, those responses become your mindset.

Words only hurt when we give them authority. When we value the speaker's opinion more than our own. When we accept judgment as truth. When we internalize negativity that was never meant to nurture us.

Take that authority away, and the words lose their power. Criticism becomes information—or noise. Insults reveal more about the speaker than about you. You were not injured by what was said; you were affected by what you allowed it to mean.

This does not mean pretending that words don't matter, or suppressing emotion when pain arises. It means choosing awareness over impulse. It means understanding that your inner peace is not something others can steal—it is something you govern.

When you stop outsourcing your self-worth, you stop giving people the power to wound you.

You are not weak for feeling hurt. But you become strong when you realize you don't have to stay there.

No one controls your inner world unless you hand them the keys. Guard your peace. Choose your responses.

Because your power begins exactly where your permission ends.

Day 92 — Study Your Emotions

Emotions are not interruptions to life. They are part of life itself.

From the moment we are born, emotions guide us. An infant cannot explain what it feels, yet it communicates clearly—through crying, smiling, clinging, or laughter. Long before words appear, emotions speak. As we grow, we gain something powerful: the ability not just to *feel*, but to *understand* what we feel.

That ability is called emotional awareness.

To study your emotions means learning to pause and notice what is happening inside you. It means recognizing the feeling, naming it honestly, and gently asking why it has appeared. Instead of being swept away by emotion, you begin to observe it.

This small shift changes everything.

When emotions are noticed early, they lose the power to control behavior unconsciously. You respond instead of react. You gain space between stimulus and action. Over time, this awareness becomes the foundation of emotional intelligence—a skill closely tied to healthy relationships, leadership, wise decisions, and inner stability.

Emotions are temporary by nature. Some pass in seconds. Others linger and turn into moods. They vary in intensity, but none of them are wrong. There are no "bad" emotions—only messages that need interpretation. Even uncomfortable feelings carry useful information about your needs, values, and boundaries.

Most emotional suffering comes not from the emotion itself, but from judging it.

"I shouldn't feel this way." "I shouldn't be angry." "I shouldn't be scared."

Judgment creates resistance. Resistance strengthens the emotion.

Awareness, on the other hand, allows emotion to move through you naturally. When a feeling is noticed and named, it often softens on its own. Suppression traps emotion. Observation releases it.

Emotions influence nearly every decision you make—whether you realize it or not. Anger pushes confrontation. Fear urges avoidance. Love draws closeness. Joy fuels creativity. Even decisions that appear logical are colored by emotional states beneath the surface.

This is why early thinkers understood emotions as tools for survival. They help us bond, protect ourselves, communicate, and adapt. Emotions are not flaws in human design—they are part of its intelligence.

Studying your emotions is not self-indulgence. It is self-mastery.

When you understand what you feel, you communicate more clearly, manage conflict more calmly, and navigate life with greater balance. You stop fighting yourself and start learning from yourself.

Your emotions are not enemies to defeat. They are messages to understand.

Don't judge them. Don't suppress them. Notice them. Name them. Learn from them.

That quiet practice is where emotional intelligence—and inner strength—begins.

Day 93 — Your Thoughts Create Your Reality

Thoughts, by themselves, are harmless. They become powerful only when we give them our attention.

A thought appears quietly in the mind. If we ignore it, it fades. But if we replay it, believe it, or worry about it, it begins to feel real. That single act of attention is what gives a thought its strength. Soon, it triggers an emotion. The emotion alters how the body feels and responds. And from that inner state, behavior naturally follows. Over time, those behaviors shape the experiences we call *reality*.

This is how thoughts, unseen and unnoticed, begin to build our lives.

Every day, your inner world moves in a simple but powerful cycle: you think, you feel, you act, and then you experience the results of those actions. Those results often confirm the original thought, and the cycle repeats. Slowly, quietly, this loop becomes automatic.

This is why two people can live in the same environment yet experience completely different realities. The situation may be identical, but the interpretation is not. Life does not affect us directly—we experience life through the lens of thought.

Over time, repeated thoughts form patterns. Patterns become habits of thinking. Habits of thinking harden into beliefs. And beliefs begin to run on autopilot. Neuroscience explains this simply: what we repeatedly think strengthens neural pathways. The mind becomes efficient at thinking the same way again and again.

That efficiency can work for us—or against us.

Once a belief is formed, the mind starts filtering reality to match it. Evidence that supports the belief is highlighted. Evidence that contradicts it is ignored. This is why beliefs feel so real, even when they are limiting or untrue. We are not seeing reality as it is—we are seeing reality as we believe it to be.

Think of your mind as a garden.

Every thought is a seed. Some seeds are nourishing—confidence, patience, gratitude, curiosity. Others are toxic—fear, self-doubt, resentment, hopelessness. You may not control which seeds land in the garden, but you do control which ones you water. Whatever you give attention to grows.

And here is the most liberating truth of all: you are not your thoughts.

You are the one who notices them. You are the one who chooses which thoughts to engage with and which to let pass.

Your outer world is shaped from the inside out. Change does not begin by fixing life—it begins by observing thought.

When you stop believing every thought that passes through your mind, you regain choice. And with choice comes freedom.

You are the thinker. You are the gardener. Choose your thoughts wisely—because over time, they quietly become your reality.

Day 94 — Change Requires Action

We often say we want change. We want to be healthier, more confident, more successful, more fulfilled. The desire is sincere. The intention is real. Yet, for many people, life remains exactly the same.

Not because change is impossible— but because change is never passive.

If you want a stronger body, you must move it. If you want a better job, you must apply. If you want a new skill, you must practice. If you want to write a book, you must sit down and write—slowly, imperfectly, one line at a time.

There is no other way.

Most people do not stay stuck because they lack dreams. They stay stuck because they wait. They wait for confidence, clarity, motivation, or the "right moment." But life rarely provides perfect conditions.

Change does not begin with certainty. It begins with willingness.

Life improves not when we think about doing something, but when we actually do it. Progress responds only to action. Without it, nothing shifts—no matter how strong the intention.

You are not a spectator in your life. You are the author.

And if you want a different chapter, you must write it differently. Wishing will not rewrite the story. Hoping will not move the plot forward. Only action creates momentum.

Even small steps matter. Especially small steps.

Fear often feels like the reason we don't act. In truth, fear grows when we stay still. The moment we take action—any action—fear begins to weaken. Clarity replaces confusion. Confidence slowly replaces doubt.

You don't act because you feel ready. You feel ready because you act.

Change is not something you wait for. It is something you create.

Start where you are. Begin with what you can. Take one honest step today.

Because change doesn't happen *to* you. It happens *through* you.

Day 95 — The Future Is Not Defined by the Past or the Present

Your past may explain parts of you, but it does not own you. It may have shaped your thinking, tested your strength, or slowed your progress—but it does not get to decide where your life goes next.

We are all influenced by what we have lived through. That is human. But influence is not imprisonment. Painful experiences are not verdicts. Difficult beginnings are not permanent identities. They are chapters—nothing more.

Hard times do not exist to label us. They exist to train us.

The past is meant to be a teacher, not a judge. If yesterday truly controlled tomorrow, growth would be impossible. People would remain forever stuck in the place they started or the mistakes they once made. Yet history—and everyday life—prove otherwise.

Like a lotus that rises from muddy water and blooms untouched by the dirt beneath it, human beings have the capacity to grow out of difficulty with strength and clarity.

Your past is not your destiny. Your past is not your limitation. Your past is not your sentence.

What often separates those who move forward from those who remain stuck is not intelligence or luck—but focus.

Some people live in old stories, replaying what went wrong, what was unfair, or what they lost. Over time, the past becomes a weight they carry everywhere. Responsibility fades. Hope weakens. And without realizing it, they recreate the same future again and again.

Others do something different. They accept what happened—and then act from where they are.

Responsibility is not blame. Responsibility is freedom.

You may not control how your story began. But you always control how the next page is written. Every choice you make today matters. Every action you take now is a vote for the future you are building.

Yesterday cannot be changed. Tomorrow can be designed.

If your present feels disappointing, remember this: it is not permanent. It is not final. And it is not a reflection of everything you are capable of becoming.

The moment you choose awareness over regret, action over replay, and responsibility over resignation—you take your power back.

Your future is not written by where you've been, nor by where you stand today.

It is written by what you choose to do next.

Let the past inform you—but never imprison you. Let the present challenge you—but never define you. Your best chapters are still waiting to be written.

Day 96 — Staying Where You Are Is Falling Behind

In a world that is constantly moving forward, standing still is not neutral. If you choose not to move, you do not remain where you are—you quietly fall behind.

Life today moves like an airport's moving walkway. If you stand still while others walk, you may still be moving—but far more slowly than everyone else. And the moment the walkway stops, so do you. Progress requires effort. Stillness may feel safe, but it carries a silent cost.

Comfort is persuasive. Familiar routines demand no courage. Old habits do not question your identity. The status quo does not ask you to risk failure, embarrassment, or discomfort. It gently whispers, *"This is good enough."*

Growth, however, asks uncomfortable questions. Can this be improved? What am I avoiding? What do I need to learn next?

When comfort is chosen repeatedly over growth, stagnation slowly sets in.

Stagnation often hides behind complacency. It looks like dissatisfaction without action, complaints without change, and blame without responsibility. It shows up as doing just enough to get by, while secretly hoping life will improve on its own. Complacency does not announce failure loudly—it fades quietly through missed opportunities, outdated skills, and lost relevance.

The world does not pause for anyone.

Industries evolve. Expectations rise. Skills that once mattered slowly lose value. What worked yesterday may not work tomorrow. Many people do not fall behind because they lack ability—but because they stop adapting.

Growth is no longer optional. It is necessary.

This truth is especially important for leaders—at work and in life. Leadership is not about maintaining comfort. It is about forward motion. Progress comes from asking difficult questions, seeking improvement, and refusing to settle into stagnation.

There is a simple truth beneath it all: You are always in one of two states—moving forward or falling behind. There is no pause button.

Growth does not require dramatic change or giant leaps. It requires consistency. Learning a little more. Improving a little each day. Adjusting when needed. Even small steps keep you relevant. Even small effort compounds over time.

Do not aim to stay comfortable. Aim to stay growing.
In a fast-moving world, standing still feels safe—but it quietly costs you everything. Choose progress. Because staying where you are is the slowest way to move backward.

Day 97 — Teach Yourself Every Day

If you look closely at the most successful people in the world, one pattern quietly repeats itself. What sets them apart is not extraordinary talent or luck—it is their commitment to learning. They keep acquiring new skills, new ideas, and new ways of thinking. While others switch their minds off through constant distraction, they invest small pockets of time in expanding their understanding.

Teaching yourself every day does not require classrooms, degrees, or dramatic changes. It doesn't mean quitting your job to attend long courses or locking yourself away with textbooks. Real learning is subtle. It is practical. It blends into daily life through curiosity, reflection, and attention.

Opportunities to learn are everywhere—if you are willing to notice them.

Children learn effortlessly because they experiment without fear. They ask questions freely. They explore without worrying about being wrong. As adults, we often lose this openness. We dismiss new ideas too quickly or assume we already know enough. Returning to a childlike curiosity—asking *why* and *how* without judgment—reopens the door to learning.

Mistakes play a powerful role in self-education. When life is viewed only through results, mistakes feel like failure. But when viewed through growth, mistakes become information. They show you what doesn't work and where refinement is needed. Every error carries a lesson—if you are willing to examine it rather than escape it.

Routine, while comforting, can quietly dull the mind. Breaking patterns refreshes perception. Taking a different route, having lunch with someone new, or stepping outside familiar environments introduces new ideas. Growth often comes from unexpected conversations and unfamiliar experiences.

Learning also depends on what you feed your mind. Podcasts, books, articles, thoughtful videos, and conversations—all shape your thinking. When you explore ideas beyond your comfort zone, assumptions loosen and understanding deepens. Mastery grows faster when fundamentals are solid, and learning becomes easier when it builds upon interests you already enjoy.

The reason daily learning matters is simple. The world is changing faster than ever. Skills expire. Certainty fades. In such a world, the greatest advantage is not knowing everything—but remaining adaptable.

The brain is like a muscle. Neglect weakens it. Gentle, consistent use strengthens it. Learning something new each day—even something small—keeps the mind sharp, flexible, and resilient.

You don't need to know everything. You only need to stay teachable.

Ask yourself one quiet question at the end of each day: *What did I learn today?*

That single habit—repeated daily—has the power to change not just what you know, but who you become.

Day 98 — Sometimes the Whole Story Is Just a Chapter

The story of your life is not a single moment—it is a book written one chapter at a time. And one difficult chapter does not decide how the book will end.

Our lives unfold like stories. Some chapters are light and joyful, easy to read and easy to remember. Others are heavy, confusing, and painful. But no reader closes a book forever because one chapter feels difficult. They keep reading—because they understand that every story needs contrast, tension, and turning points.

Life works the same way.

Think of a long journey. Every traveler encounters rough stretches—detours, delays, broken roads, unexpected obstacles. No one turns back just because one part of the road is difficult. They slow down, adjust their route, and continue forward. A difficult phase is not a dead end; it is simply a section of the road you are currently walking.

When you are inside a hard chapter, it can feel endless. Pain has a way of convincing us that it will last forever. But pain lies. What feels permanent in the moment is almost always temporary in hindsight. What hurts today becomes perspective tomorrow.

Do not tear out the difficult chapters. Those pages carry lessons you could not learn any other way. Strength is often built quietly, in moments when nothing seems to be working. And many times, the chapters we once wished away become the ones that give the story its depth and meaning.

Smooth stories are rarely memorable. Growth comes from contrast. Wisdom comes from experience. And resilience is shaped in chapters we never planned to write.

Life does not stop because one chapter is hard. It keeps moving forward, whether we resist it or not. As someone once wisely observed, life goes on—and so must you.

Your life is still being written. A single chapter cannot decide the ending.

Keep turning the pages. Keep showing up. Because often, the best chapters come *after* the hardest ones.

Day 99 — Choose Your Battles Wisely

Choosing your battles means being intentional about where you invest your time, energy, and emotional strength. It is not about avoiding problems or running away from challenges—it is about recognizing which struggles deserve your attention and which ones quietly drain you without adding value.

Not every issue requires a response. Not every disagreement deserves your energy. And not every confrontation leads to growth.

Winning every argument is not the same as winning in life. Often, the urge to prove a point costs us something far more valuable—peace, focus, and clarity. Wisdom lies in knowing when to speak, when to act, and when to step back without guilt.

Many things that disturb us today will not matter tomorrow. When you look five, ten, or twenty years ahead, most daily irritations shrink into insignificance. Yet we spend precious mental and emotional energy reacting to moments that leave no lasting impact on our lives.

Every battle you choose to fight has a cost. Even when you "win," the question remains—was the victory worth the time, mental space, and emotional effort it consumed? Time is limited. Energy is limited. Attention is limited. Choosing your battles is, in truth, choosing how you live your life.

Wise people are strategic with their energy. Before reacting, they pause and ask themselves: Does this matter in the long run? Will engaging move my life forward—or pull me away from what truly matters?

Most negativity does not need to be confronted. It needs to be ignored.

Like the elephant who stepped aside rather than step into the mud, strength is not always shown through force. Sometimes it is shown through restraint—not because you are weak, but because you value your peace more than your ego.

You don't need to fight every battle to prove your strength. Some battles are won the moment you choose not to engage.

Protect your peace. Save your energy. Choose only the battles that move your life forward— because knowing what to ignore is one of life's greatest victories.

Day 100 — Attention Is the New Currency

Never in history have we been more connected to the world—and yet, paradoxically, less connected to ourselves and to one another. Technology has transformed how we work, communicate, and live. But its most powerful impact has been subtle and invisible: it has reshaped how we pay attention.

Information now floods our lives without pause. Messages arrive before we are ready. Notifications interrupt our thoughts. Headlines demand urgency. Videos autoplay. Social media pulls us into endless scrolling. Our minds are stretched across too many places at once. The result is not progress, but exhaustion. We feel busy all day, yet strangely unfulfilled—productive on the surface, scattered underneath.

The problem is not a lack of time.
The problem is a loss of control over attention.

Time has always been limited. Attention is even more precious. Time simply passes; attention is chosen. Where you place it decides how that time shapes your life.

Think of attention as currency. Spend it carelessly, and you are left empty—no matter how much time you had. Spend it intentionally, and even a small amount creates immense value. We now live in an attention economy. Everything around us is designed to capture and hold our focus. Apps are engineered to be addictive. News cycles thrive on outrage. Entertainment competes for seconds, not depth.

The most valuable—and most endangered—resource of the modern age is human attention.

Every day, more content is created than any individual could consume in a lifetime. Information overload is no longer an exception; it is the default state of life. And if you do not consciously decide where your attention goes, something else will decide for you.

Reclaiming attention does not mean rejecting technology or withdrawing from the world. It means becoming deliberate. It means choosing rather than reacting.

Each day begins better when you ask one quiet but powerful question:
What truly deserves my attention today?

When that question is answered honestly, distractions lose much of their power.

Clarity creates focus. Structure protects energy. When everything feels urgent, nothing is truly important. But when priorities are defined, attention naturally aligns. Purpose gives direction to focus.

Technology must also be put back in its rightful place. It is a tool—useful, powerful, and efficient—but a dangerous master. Every platform is designed to keep you engaged, not fulfilled. Used consciously, technology serves you. Used unconsciously, it slowly consumes you.

Equally important is something we often forget in a culture obsessed with speed: focus cannot survive without rest.

We move faster than ever before. Tasks compress. Expectations multiply. Without pause, the mind overheats. Burnout is not a failure of effort—it is a failure of recovery. Rest is not laziness; it is maintenance. Just as muscles grow stronger during rest, clarity and creativity emerge when the mind is allowed to slow down.

In the end, the truth is quiet but undeniable.

Where you place your attention shapes what you achieve, who you become, and how meaningful your life feels. The world will always compete for your focus. That will never change.

But protecting your attention—that responsibility is yours.

Attention is the new currency.
Spend it wisely. Guard it fiercely.

Because when you control your attention, you don't just manage your time— you reclaim your life.

Day 101 — For Every Level, There Is Another Devil

With every new level we reach in life, a new challenge is already waiting—not loudly, not dramatically, but patiently. These challenges are not punishments, nor signs that something has gone wrong. They exist because growth always asks for more. Each level prepares us for the next, and preparation is rarely comfortable.

Life, in this way, is much like the video games we play. As we move ahead, the levels become harder. New challenges appear. Old strategies stop working. What once required little effort now demands focus, skill, and discipline. But the game does not become harder because we are failing—it becomes harder because we are progressing.

Growth does not remove difficulty; it reshapes it.

At early levels of life, challenges are obvious and external—lack of experience, uncertainty, limited resources. As we advance, the obstacles grow quieter and more internal. The battles shift from the outside to the inside: patience, self-control, consistency, and responsibility. The enemies become subtler, but the stakes become higher.

Every step forward introduces a new kind of resistance.

If you want a higher level of success, you must accept a higher level of responsibility. In a game, reaching a new level unlocks tougher opponents and greater risks. In life, it unlocks deeper expectations. What you gain outwardly must be matched by what you strengthen inwardly.

Every level has its own "devil," and it rarely looks the way we expect. Sometimes it is fear. Sometimes it is comfort. Sometimes it is the temptation to stay where things feel manageable. Avoidance keeps us stuck on old levels. Progress requires the courage to face what stands in the way.

The next phase of life will always demand a new version of you—clearer thinking, deeper discipline, greater emotional maturity. When pressure appears, when doubt surfaces, when obstacles feel unfair, it is easy to assume something has gone wrong. Often, it is a sign that you have entered a new level.

Many people admire growth but underestimate its cost. They want advancement without resistance, success without struggle. But growth works the same way every meaningful game does: difficulty increases because the player has grown stronger.

Each level refines you quietly. Your perspective sharpens. Your resilience deepens. Your understanding becomes steadier. Growth is not merely about reaching higher—it is about becoming capable of staying there.

For every level, there is another devil.

Do not fear it. Face it with awareness and patience. Because every challenge you overcome unlocks the next level—and the next version of you.

Still Becoming

If you have reached this page, pause for a moment—not because the journey is over, but because you stayed with it.

This book was never meant to be completed in the traditional sense, but returned to. One page at a time. One thought at a time. One honest reflection at a time.

Growth rarely announces itself. It arrives quietly—through awareness, discipline, patience, perspective, and clarity. Through days when you showed up fully, and days when simply showing up was enough. Through chapters that resonated deeply and others that challenged you uncomfortably. All of it mattered.

You may not feel transformed in dramatic ways—and that is a good sign. Real growth is subtle. It reshapes how you respond, how you pause, how you listen to yourself and to others. It changes the quality of your inner conversations long before it changes external outcomes.

Remember this: becoming is not a destination. It is a lifelong process.

There will be days ahead when you feel certain, and days when clarity feels distant again. There will be new challenges, new beginnings, and chapters you never anticipated. When that happens, return to what you already know now—that growth happens one chapter at a time.

You do not need to rush.
You do not need to compare.
You do not need to have it all figured out.

You only need to keep becoming—honestly, patiently, and intentionally.

This may be the final page of this book, but it is not the final chapter of your story.

Turn the page.
Live the lesson.
And continue becoming.

Acknowledgements

This book exists because of many unseen contributions—some spoken, many silent.

I begin with gratitude for the people who crossed my path at different stages of my journey. Some stayed, some moved on, and some appeared only briefly—but each left behind a lesson that shaped my thinking, resilience, and growth. Every conversation, challenge, encouragement, and setback became a quiet teacher, guiding me in ways I did not always recognize at the time.

I am deeply thankful to the communities that gave me the space to practice, reflect, and evolve—especially the platforms where these thoughts first found their voice. Writing daily reflections and sharing them consistently was not easy, but the process itself became my greatest education. The discipline of showing up, thinking deeply, and articulating honestly transformed not only my communication, but my mindset.

To my mentors, seniors, colleagues, and peers—thank you for your guidance, patience, feedback, and belief. Some of you taught through advice, others through example, and a few simply by asking the right questions at the right time. Each influence helped refine my perspective and strengthen my resolve.

To my family, thank you for being my constant anchor. Your quiet support, understanding, and trust gave me the freedom to grow at my own pace. Your belief in me often arrived before my own—and for that, I am deeply grateful.

My deepest gratitude to my wife, whose steady presence made this journey possible in ways that often go unnoticed. By taking care of life's everyday routines and responsibilities, she created the mental space that allowed me to remain curious, engaged, and creative. Her patience, understanding, and quiet strength kept me grounded and focused, even on days when inspiration wavered.

I am also grateful to my son for his creative inputs in shaping the cover design of this book, and for encouraging me to bring these reflections together in a form that could be shared.

A special note of love and gratitude to my angel daughter, whose innocent warmth and pampering affection fill my days with joy and remind me of the simple beauty of presence.

To every reader who has paused, reflected, and chosen to grow alongside these pages—thank you. This book is as much yours as it is mine. If even one chapter helped you slow down, think differently, or move forward with greater clarity, then this journey has been worthwhile.

Finally, I acknowledge myself—for staying consistent, for continuing despite doubt, and for choosing growth over comfort. This book stands as a reminder that progress is possible when we commit to showing up, one chapter at a time.

With gratitude,

Manish Manohar

About the Author

Manish Manohar works as a **Company Secretary and Law Officer** in a **Central Public Sector Enterprise**, based in Assam, in the serene and culturally rich Northeast region of India. His professional journey is rooted in **Corporate Governance and Law**, shaped by discipline, responsibility, and a sustained commitment to ethical clarity.

An Aquarian by nature and a non-believer in conventional notions of God, Manish believes that the divine resides as a conscious soul within the human body. In his view, each individual carries the responsibility of nurturing the body and mind—to remain balanced, aware, and inwardly aligned.

He is a law graduate from **Symbiosis Law School, Pune**, and a member of the **Institute of Cost and Management Accountants of India (ICMAI)** and the **Institute of Company Secretaries of India (ICSI)**. He is also an alumnus of the **National Institute of Bank Management (NIBM), Pune**.

Beyond his professional life, Manish has served as **President of a Toastmasters Club**, an experience that deepened his engagement with reflective communication, mindful expression, and the discipline of articulating thought with clarity and purpose.

A lifelong learner with a quiet yet unwavering pursuit of growth, Manish writes not from borrowed theory, but from lived experience. His reflections emerge from observation, failure, resilience, and daily practice. Through his writing, he seeks clarity, self-awareness, and conscious living—approaching life, and growth, **one chapter at a time**.